Praise for *Make a D*

"In *Make a Difference*, Arthur Blaustein cuts through public cynicism about ideals like government and service, not just challenging Americans to fulfill the role of 'citizen'—a nation's highest calling—but offering both a blueprint and guidebook to help us all get involved. If you ask most people what the most memorable phrase of the past fifty years is, a majority will probably tell you it is President Kennedy's words: 'Ask not what your country can do for you; ask what you can do for your country.' Blaustein's effort will help a new generation of Americans approach community service—and their own lives—in a way that will strengthen our democracy and help reclaim that special idealism of which President Kennedy spoke."

—SENATOR JOHN KERRY

"*Make a Difference* is an exceptional contribution to our nation's civic life. It is a terrific resource. By listing so many organizations, along with their descriptions and contact information, Arthur Blaustein has made it easy for every citizen to volunteer. I applaud the exhaustive research and work that has gone into this valuable book."

—BOB CHASE, PRESIDENT, NATIONAL EDUCATION ASSOCIATION

"Wouldn't you like help in making September 11th a transformative event? Blaustein's book is perfectly timed to help us resist a return to the alienating privatism that has robbed us of the traditions of civic membership. A perfect graduation gift—for us all!"—GAIL SHEEHY, AUTHOR OF THE *PASSAGES* BOOKS

"An excellent compilation for readers hoping to improve society through service. This book makes finding volunteering opportunities easier than ever—it should be read by all people looking for creative and useful ways to benefit communities across America."—SENATOR EDWARD M. KENNEDY

"Congratulations to Arthur Blaustein for giving America an important book that our citizens need now more than ever. Volunteering and community service are the heart of our nation, and *Make a Difference* shows us how to become an active part of this wonderful tradition."

—WILLIAM FERRIS, FORMER CHAIR,
NATIONAL ENDOWMENT FOR THE HUMANITIES

"*Make a Difference* is a clear and compelling account of why civic responsibility and citizen participation are essential to the health and vitality of American democracy. Blaustein provides an excellent guide to using our energy, patriotism, and compassion for the benefit of our communities and our country."

—SENATOR TOM DASCHLE, MAJORITY LEADER, UNITED STATES SENATE

MAKE A DIFFERENCE

YOUR GUIDE TO VOLUNTEERING AND COMMUNITY SERVICE

Arthur I. Blaustein

HEYDAY BOOKS • BERKELEY, CALIFORNIA

Library of Congress Cataloging-in-Publication Data

Blaustein, Arthur I.
  Make a difference : your guide to volunteering and community service /
by Arthur I. Blaustein.
      p. cm.
Includes bibliographical references and index.
  ISBN 1-890771-55-4 (pbk. : alk. paper)

  1. Voluntarism—United States—Directories. I. Title.
  HN90.V64 B53 2002
  361.3'7—dc21

                                        2002001182

Cover/ Interior Design: Rebecca LeGates
Printing and Binding: Banta Book Group, Menasha, WI

Orders, inquiries, and correspondence should be addressed to:
      Heyday Books
      P. O. Box 9145, Berkeley, CA 94709
      (510) 549-3564, Fax (510) 549-1889
      www.heydaybooks.com

Printed in the United States of America

10 9 8 7 6 5 4 3 2 1

To my students

"The good we secure for ourselves is precarious and uncertain...until it is secured for all of us and incorporated into our common life."
—Jane Addams

"We make a living by what we get, but we make a life by what we give."
—Winston Churchill

Contents

Acknowledgments

This book was shaped by the values I learned from teachers and mentors at different stages of my education. They taught me to think about the critical importance of moral conscience, civic responsibility, and community service. I am especially indebted to William Casey (Columbia University), Dorothy Dulles Bourne (Bard College), Miss Fox (fourth grade, P.S. 70, NYC), Allen Wheelis, and Dr. Morris Blaustein (my father).

I can't possibly mention all of those friends and colleagues whose encouragement and assistance allowed me to undertake and complete this book; but I do want to give special thanks to some whose recent support was crucial. Darol Ryan and Debbie Berne provided valuable research assistance; Judy MacLean's common sense and editorial skills added clarity and conciseness to what I wanted to say; and Lisa Bornstein is an extraordinary copy editor and valued counsel. Stan and Sydney Shuman's friendship and gracious hospitality provided the space to allow me to conceive and design this project. In various ways and at critical times, Megan Voorhees, Marge Allen, Sabrina Bornstein, Sandra Brod, Chandra Egan, Clay Felker, Allen Horne, and Erin Kelley provided helpful assistance and useful suggestions.

This book is a product of the collaboration of author and publisher. Malcolm Margolin's keen insights, editorial suggestions, and genuine enthusiasm were indispensable. I am also indebted to the staff at Heyday Books, particularly Ani Chamichian, Jeannine Gendar, Rebecca LeGates, Karen Lichtenberg, Lisa K. Manwill, Victoria Root, Patricia Wakida, and Maureen Watts, whose invaluable efforts have contributed to making this a better book.

The one shortcoming of the book is the lack of space to include the many other deserving organizations that are doing a superb job of serving our communities. Hopefully, more of them can be included in the next edition.

Part 1:
The Challenge of
Community Service

The traditions of community service and citizen participation have been at the heart of American civic culture since before the nation was founded; whether through town hall meetings, the local school board, a political party, a hospital auxiliary, or one of our innumerable other national and local organizations, Americans have felt and acted on the need to give something back to their communities. Yet since the events of September 11, this need has become more urgent, as Americans on the whole have become more introspective and more patriotic. This patriotism has taken many different forms, but one thing is clear: our concern for our country, our communities, our families, and our neighbors has become more acute, and our need to contribute more urgent.

With firefighters, police officers, and rescue teams leading the way, ordinary citizens—ironworkers, teachers, public health clinicians, professionals, businesspeople, and schoolchildren—either volunteered to go to ground zero or offered their support from a distance. Everything from blankets to blood, peanut butter to poetry arrived in New York City by the bale, the gallon, the barrel, and the ream. Americans didn't wait until January 1, 2002, to make resolutions; in mid-September, many resolved to be more caring and giving.

Make a Difference is here to help harness this outpouring of compassion, energy, and patriotism in creative and useful ways. If you've decided to make a difference because of the events of September 11, or if volunteering is one of those things you've been meaning to do all along but just haven't gotten around to, or if you're just curious about what's out there, this book can help you take the next step. It was designed to help you decide that you can make a contribution to the well-being of your community. It will help to answer the why, the how, the what, and the when. Why is community service important? How can you get in touch with a group that promotes the values and goals that you believe in? What specific volunteer activities match up with your skills and experiences? When is a good time to volunteer?

Each of the organizations included in the book has been selected because of its commitment to educational, social, economic, environmental, and community development goals. Some have been in existence for many decades and others are fairly new. Most are national organizations and some are local prototypes; but all have a solid track record of delivering services that are useful and meaningful. Before you select an organization, ask yourself a few questions.

How much time do you want to serve?
What kind of service fits your personality?
What neighborhood and community do you want to work in?
Which target population do you want to work with?
What skills do you have to offer?
What would you like to gain from the experience?

If, for example, you're over seventeen, can commit a full year, and would like leadership training, some income, and a stipend, you should seriously consider AmeriCorps. If you want to commit a year and you're over eighteen and want to work on environmental, art, or music projects, or in community development, you should think about Volunteers in Service to America (VISTA). If you only have a weekend or one day a week, you like working with your hands, and you want to be outdoors, Habitat for Humanity will probably be perfect. If you only have a few hours a week and enjoy children, consider mentoring or tutoring with an educational group. It might take some reflection and research, but there *is* a fulfilling opportunity for everyone.

Historically, our greatest strength as a nation has been to be there for one another. Citizen participation is the lifeblood of democracy. As Thomas Paine put it, "The highest calling of every individual in a democratic society is that of citizen!" Accidents of nature and abstract notions of improvement do not make our communities better or healthier places in which to live and work. They get better because people like you decide that they want to make a difference.

Volunteering is not a conservative or liberal, Democratic or Republican issue; caring and compassion simply help to define us as being human. Unfortunately, opportunistic radio talk-show hosts and reactionary politicians have spread two false myths about community service. The first is the notion that only inner-city minorities benefit from volunteer efforts. Here's a story about that myth, told to me by a friend who was in VISTA. He was helping local groups organize fuel cooperatives many years ago, in small towns in Maine. That winter was unusually cold and the price of home heating had skyrocketed, placing an enormous financial burden on most families in the state, which had a low per-capita income. He was invited to make a presentation to about two hundred residents in their town's church. After the talk, one of the "happy guy" television reporters from Portland baited a farmer, asking, "What do you think of this outside agitation?"

The farmer, who was about seventy-five, paused for a moment; and, with an edge of flint in his voice, he said, "You know, I'm a fourth-generation Republican Yankee—just like my father, my grandfather, and my great-grandfather—but if I've learned anything, it's that there are two kinds of politics and economics in America. The first kind is what I see on television and what politicians tell me when they want my vote. The other kind is what me and my friends talk about over doughnuts and coffee. And that's what this young fellow was talking about tonight—and he made a lot of sense to me. I'm joining the co-op."

Over 65 percent of America's poor are, like this farmer, white, and white families with children are the fastest growing homeless population. The myth that social programs only serve inner-city minorities stigmatizes volunteer social programs, which are, in fact, color-blind.

The second myth is that the vast majority of individuals who volunteer for community service are naive, idealistic do-gooders. Here's a story about that myth. It happened to me in a bookstore in Northern California. Six years ago, I was a technical advisor to the producers of a public television series called "The New War on Poverty." There was a companion book to the series, and since I had been one of the contributing editors, the publisher asked me to give readings. This particular evening, I showed film clips from the series and spoke about the importance of several War on Poverty programs, including Head Start, the Job Corps, VISTA, Legal Services, and Upward Bound.

While I was signing books after the reading, a woman in her mid-twenties who looked like a quintessential California valley girl—blond hair, blue eyes—approached me with tears in her eyes. I asked if I had said anything that offended her. She replied that I had not and told me she was nonpolitical, conservative, and in her last year of law school. She had been a political science major at college but knew nothing about the history of the War on Poverty. She said she was ashamed because, despite having benefited from two of the programs I had spoken about—Head Start and Upward Bound—she had never before felt a responsibility to give back to her community, and to assure that these programs would be continued so that others could have the same opportunities she had.

Like this woman, the vast majority of volunteers I've worked with are not idealistic, but are serious realists. They are only too aware that as a nation we cannot squander our human and natural resources.

Community service not only exposes the sterility of this kind of idealism-versus-realism debate, but helps individuals to integrate their own idealism and realism. An idealist without a healthy dose of realism tends to become a naive romantic. A realist without ideals tends to become a cynic. Community service helps you put your ideals to work in a realistic setting. It creates a dynamic tension that gives you a coherent and comprehensive approach to complex problems. I've seen it happen time and again with my students, and with VISTA and AmeriCorps volunteers. Dr. Margaret Mead, one of my teachers in graduate school at Columbia, wrote that a truly healthy person is a thinking, feeling, acting person. That's what serving helps us to achieve.

The talk-show hosts and politicians who push these myths are scapegoating and attacking the most vulnerable segments of our society. They are adept at moralizing over the problems of the homeless and the hungry, the unemployed and the underemployed, drug users and the mentally ill, and over such issues as infant mortality, child and spousal abuse, and disrupted families. But they have neither the heart nor the will for rigorous thought and the work of finding cures, nor even relieving some of the suffering or symptoms. Just as military service and patriotism should not be politicized, neither should community service.

Nearly forty years ago, when President John F. Kennedy launched the Peace Corps, he made this oft-quoted suggestion: "Ask not what your country can do for you, but what you can do for your country." After thirty years of firsthand experience with hundreds of volunteers, I would make a follow-up suggestion: "Ask not what you can do for your community and the people you serve, but what they can do for you." Community service is very much a two-way street. It is about giving *and* receiving, and the receiving can be nourishing for the heart and mind. The very act of serving taps into a wellspring of empathy and generosity that is both personally gratifying and energizing. Again and again, former volunteers describe their experiences with words like these: adventure, growth, human connection, exciting, spiritual, learning, and enjoyable.

I saw this in action three years ago when I decided to give the students in each of my classes, mostly university seniors, the choice between a mid-semester exam or sixteen hours of community service. The students unanimously chose service—though most of them didn't know what was in store for them. They had a choice of about ten different activities organized by the Public Service Center at the University of California, Berkeley.

Here's what one student wrote about this experience: "Before I started volunteering, I had very different expectations about the [after-school] program. I thought it would be very sports-oriented with little academic emphasis. Luckily, my expectations proved false. The program—for fourth and fifth-graders at the Thousand Oaks/Franklin Elementary School—has a set schedule for each grade. The students rotate between free play, sports, library study time, circle time, and arts and crafts.

"It was in the library that I saw how truly behind these children are in mathematics, reading, and grammar. In addition, I never expected to see the immense poverty that these children experience or to be so emotionally affected by it. Last week, I learned that one of my favorite children is homeless. It seems so silly to be reprimanding him for not doing his homework and not putting out the effort at school. This seems so trivial compared to the real-life horrors that he must experience. Although I had my expectations, never did I anticipate the emotional attachment that I now share with these children. I find myself yearning to become a teacher, which was a career I never thought about before this program. I know that as these children grow, they will probably forget about me; but I know I will never forget them. I have truly changed and matured as a result of them."

A second student wrote: "Before I started tutoring I was really scared, because I didn't know what tutors did in junior high schools. I was afraid of not being able to explain things so that the kids could understand. I thought I might also lose patience quickly with kids who were slower in understanding and for whom I would have to repeatedly state the same thing. I was concerned that the kids would resent me or not respect me because I wasn't the teacher and was closer to their age. And finally, I thought they wouldn't like me; the first day I even had trouble introducing myself because of this initial uncertainty.

"Contrary to these preliminary fears, however, tutoring at Willard *has been a life-changing experience for me.* I've found that I have more patience working with kids than I've ever had in any other area of my life. I work hard to come up with lots of examples when the kids I'm working with don't understand. We relate well to one another because I'm close to their age, yet they respect me because I go to Cal and they know that I'm there to help them. It's been the joy of my semester to work with these students, who I really appreciate."

These comments were typical of the experiences of nearly all eighty students. Their testimony is consistent with the more formal academic research and evaluations, which tell us that service-learning clearly enriches and enhances the individual volunteer in multiple ways. And the same things happened to me during my own community service thirty-five years ago, when I taught in Harlem during the early years of the War on Poverty and VISTA.

My students now, and I back then, confronted the complexities of the everyday worlds of individuals and communities quite different from our own. We were forced to deal with difficult social and economic realities. It was an eye-opener to learn about the inequities and injustices of our society, to see firsthand the painful struggles of children who did not have the educational, social, or economic opportunities that we took for granted. This experience was humbling and it broke down my insularity, for which I'm truly grateful. Again, it was Dr. Margaret Mead who called this "heart-learning."

Community service also taught me an important lesson about our society: ethical values and healthy communities are not inherited. They are either recreated through action by each generation, or they are not.

That is what makes AmeriCorps, VISTA, and other forms of community service unique and valuable. They help us to regenerate our best values and principles as individuals and as a society. From Plato to the present, civic virtue has been at the core of civilized behavior. My experience as a teacher and with service-learning has taught me that moral and ethical values cannot survive from one generation to the next if the only preservatives are texts or research studies. Real-life experience is the crucible for shaping values. Out of it develop an intuition and a living memory that are the seeds of a humane and just society.

The task of passing along to the young our best civic traditions is made more difficult by the steady shift of emphasis away from qualitative values (civility, cooperation, and the public interest) to quantitative ones (competition, making it, and privatism) as well as the demoralizing pursuit of mindless consumerism and trivia force-fed us by the mass media. Just about every parent and teacher I know has, in one way or another, expressed the concern that they cannot compete with the marketing techniques of the mass media, particularly television. They are worried about the potential consequences of the growing acquisitiveness, the indulgence, and the self-centeredness of children. You hear this from conservatives, liberals, and moderates. Small wonder. The average eighteen-year-old in the United States has seen more than three hundred and eighty thousand television commercials. We haven't begun to comprehend the inherent brutality of this media saturation on our children's psyches.

Materialism and assumptions of entitlement breed boredom, cynicism, drug abuse, and crime for kicks. Passivity, isolation, and depression come with television and on-line addiction. Ignorance, fear, and prejudice come from insularity and exclusivity. A national and local effort to promote community service by young people is the best antidote to these social ills. The goals are inclusive and nourishing; they seek to honor diversity, to protect the environment, and to enrich our nation's educational, social, and economic policies so that they enhance human dignity. On a personal level, volunteering—the very act of caring and doing—makes a substantial difference in our individual lives because it nourishes the moral intelligence required for critical judgment and mature behavior.

Dr. Seuss reminded us in *The Lorax* that "unless someone like you cares a whole awful lot nothing is going to get better. It's not." September 11, 2001—as tragic and traumatic as it was—can serve as a transformative event for the American people. We responded to this crisis with introspection, generosity, and caring. Now is not the time to push the snooze button and return to civic fatuity and complacency. Just as we marshaled our forces and mobilized our capacities to confront a foreign enemy, we can take action and confront our domestic problems and conflicts on the home front. In the real world, we know that taking ordinary initiatives can make a difference. It is within our power to move beyond a disaster and to create new opportunities. What it comes down to is assuming personal responsibility. If we decide to become involved in voluntary efforts, we can restore idealism, realism, responsiveness, and vitality to our institutions and our communities.

At her memorial service, it was said of Eleanor Roosevelt, the most influential American woman of the twentieth century, that "she would rather light a candle than curse the darkness." What was true for her then is true for us now. The choice to make a difference is ours.

January 2002

Part 2:
America Needs You:
Opportunities for Service

The following organizations, groups, and institutions give you an opportunity to have your voice heard and to get involved with issues you feel strongly about or want to learn more about. Each organization is listed under one of the following categories: Children; Civil Rights; Community Development and Economic Justice; Education; Environment and Sustainable Communities; Free Speech and Government Accountability; Gay and Lesbian Rights; Health Care, Hunger, and Homelessness; Human Rights; People with Disabilities; Seniors; Social Welfare and Emergency Relief; Violence Prevention and Peace; Women's Rights; and General Resource Organizations. The categories were designed to give a convenient structure to the book; we realize that many of the organizations defy categorization, as they deal with multifaceted issues, problems, and strategies. Most of the organizations listed are national and many have local and regional offices. Some are only local, and they were included because they are exemplary prototypes that can be replicated in other communities.

There is also a separate category for Issues and Policy Analysis. This section lists organizations that do not provide volunteer opportunities but do provide intelligent, up-to-date information on issues and policies that may be of interest to you.

CHILDREN

4-H

4-H (which stands for "head, heart, hands, and health") is an informal, government-linked education program and one of the largest youth organizations in the country, with a membership of nearly seven million kids. 4-H members work on a wide range of programs and projects that encompass community service, the arts, environmental education, plants and animals, science technology, earth sciences, and environmental education, among others. Established in 1902.

Volunteer Opportunities

4-H relies on adult volunteers to lead kids in projects and to help clubs stay organized and motivated. Volunteers can teach a skill (photography, computers, gardening, or public speaking, for instance), organize activity nights, special outings, or outreach projects, or assist with the general operations of a local club. 4-H clubs are organized under county extension offices.

Contact Information

Headquarters:
7100 Connecticut Avenue
Chevy Chase, MD 20815
www.4-h.org
4h-usa@reeusda.gov

America's Promise

Founded by Presidents Clinton, Bush, Carter, and Ford, with Nancy Reagan, America's Promise is an alliance of nearly 500 organizations dedicated to making America's youth a national priority. The program makes five promises: to offer young people relationships with caring adults, safe places to go after school, a healthy start, marketable skills through education, and opportunities to give back to the community. Established in 1997.

Volunteer Opportunities

America's Promise works to connect volunteers with children through nearly 500 national and local organizations.

Contact Information

Headquarters:
909 North Washington Street, Suite 400
Alexandria, VA 22314
(703) 684-4500 or (888) 55-YOUTH
www.americaspromise.org
local@americaspromise.org

Big Brothers Big Sisters of America (BBBSA)

The granddaddy of youth mentoring programs, Big Brothers was established in New York City in 1904. Joining forces with Big Sisters in 1977, BBBSA has served thousands of American kids by introducing positive relationships and caring adults into their lives. BBBSA provides ongoing support for volunteers, children, and parents or guardians. Established in 1904.

Volunteer Opportunities

Volunteers are matched in one-on-one mentoring relationships with kids. Matches can be structured in a variety of ways:

Traditional Matches—Bigs and Littles meet for weekly outings and activities. Required minimum commitment is 3 to 5 hours per week for one year.

Site-based Matches—Bigs and Littles meet at local Boys and Girls Clubs and participate together in club activities. Required minimum commitment is 2 hours per week for one year.

School-based Mentoring—Some chapters partner with local schools as sites for volunteers and kids to meet for tutoring and other activities. Required minimum commitment is one hour per week for one year.

Adult volunteers from the African American and Latino communities are especially needed.

Contact Information

Headquarters:
230 North 13th Street
Philadelphia, PA 19107
(215) 567-7000
www.bbbsa.org
national@bbbsa.org

Children Now

Using the media to bring attention to children's issues, Children Now disseminates information and encourages action on behalf of America's youth. Particularly concerned with children's health issues, the organization advocates for universal health coverage for American children. Established in 1988.

Volunteer Opportunities

Children Now utilizes volunteers for research, marketing, and administrative help on a per-project basis in one of four departments: communication, policy, media, and development. Interested persons are encouraged to send a letter of interest by mail or email.

Contact Information

1212 Broadway, Fifth floor
Oakland, CA 94612
(510) 763-2444
www.childrennow.org
children@childrennow.org

Children's Defense Fund (CDF)

"Leave No Child Behind" is the motto and mission of CDF, which advocates on behalf of American children, paying particular attention to the needs of poor, minority, and disabled kids. Areas of activism include health care, early education, child poverty and parental employment, violence prevention, youth development, mental health, and faith. Established in 1973.

Volunteer Opportunities

CDF welcomes volunteers to offer administrative support in their Washington, DC office. Duties include database management, mailings, and communicating with children's advocates across the nation, as well as filing, copying, faxing, and other office duties. Volunteers are also utilized in regional, state, and local offices.

Contact Information

Headquarters:
25 E Street NW
Washington, DC 20001
(202) 628-8787
www.childrensdefense.org

Court Appointed Special Advocates (CASA)

CASA provides volunteer advocates to abused and neglected children in the court system. By working closely on individual cases, community volunteers provide thorough background information and independent recommendations, and represent the best interests of a child within the child welfare system. Established in 1977.

Volunteer Opportunities

CASA is entirely volunteer-based. Volunteers become intimately involved in the details of court-assigned cases, researching the history and background of an individual case and conducting interviews with everyone involved. Most CASA programs ask for a minimum commitment of one year, although some cases will last longer. CASA volunteers give an average of 88 hours of service per year. CASA provides thorough training to all volunteers on issues of the court process, child development, abuse and neglect, cultural competency, advocacy, interviewing techniques, and HIV and other public health topics. Volunteers are recruited through over 800 local chapters across the country.

Contact information

Headquarters:
100 West Harrison
North Tower, Suite 500
Seattle, WA 98119
(800) 628-3233
www.nationalcasa.org

Make-A-Wish Foundation

Make-A-Wish Foundation grants the wishes of children with life-threatening illnesses. Since its founding, the Foundation has fulfilled more than 80,000 dreams and counting. Established in 1980.

Volunteer Opportunities

There are more than 80 chapters of Make-A-Wish in the United States, staffing more than 20,000 volunteers. Volunteers are needed for wish-granting, development and fund-raising, special events, marketing, public relations and advertising, translation services, medical outreach, website design, and general administration. All volunteer organizing is done at the local level.

Contact Information

Headquarters:
3550 North Central Avenue, Suite 300
Phoenix, AZ 85012
(800) 722-WISH or (602) 279-WISH
www.wish.org
mawfa@wish.org

After graduating from the University of Utah and doing graduate work in education, I served as a team leader in the National Civilian Community Corps. My team served in projects as varied as supporting teams at the World Special Olympics in North Carolina and rehabilitating basements in Grand Forks, North Dakota.

Being a volunteer and serving in several different communities was a phenomenal experience. My team was great; we became a family of sorts as we traveled all over the country in a fifteen-passenger van. Each project provided a new challenge and the opportunity to meet amazing people who were serving others and/or preserving the environment. We had the unique opportunity to live and work in different communities during our term of service, and that was our greatest privilege.

—Alexis Bucknam

CIVIL RIGHTS

Asian Americans for Community Outreach (AACO)

AACO brings together volunteers in a variety of community service projects, charity fundraisers, and social events. Their goal: have fun, raise money, and promote awareness of social and political issues relevant to the Asian American community. Members are professionals and students in their 20s and 30s. Established in 1994.

Volunteer Opportunities

AACO sponsors a broad range of one-time volunteer opportunities in the San Francisco Bay Area. Individuals might help staff booths at local cultural festivals such as the Chinese New Year or the Cherry Blossom Festival, volunteer at food banks or shelters, or participate in a haunted house to benefit foster children. AACO also hosts an annual Sports Day charity tournament and holiday gift drive.

Contact Information

P.O. Box 61384
Sunnyvale, CA 94008
www.aaco-sf.org
info@aaco-sf.org

Coalition for Immigrants' Rights at the Community Level (CIRCLE)

CIRCLE provides legal and support services for immigrants (and their families) detained by the INS (Immigration and Naturalization Service) at York County Prison. CIRCLE is particularly attuned to the needs of asylum seekers who may be fleeing persecution in their home countries. CIRCLE provides visitors and pen pals for those in detention, assistance with release planning and integration into the community, and legal counsel. Established in 2000.

Volunteer Opportunities

CIRCLE accepts short- and long-term volunteers to help in a variety of capacities, including attending immigration hearings, researching country conditions and case law, visiting detainees, becoming pen pals, and providing transportation and administrative and moral support. Medical, legal, and psychological professionals are especially needed to conduct exams and evaluations for use in the courts.

Contact Information

140 Roosevelt Avenue, Suite 202
York, PA 17404
(717) 845-5509
http://hometown.aol.com/circleyork
circleyork@aol.com

Disability Rights Education and Defense Fund (DREDF)

DREDF works to secure and promote the civil rights of people with disabilities. They have been involved in almost every disability rights case argued in front of the U.S. Supreme Court and were instrumental in gaining passage of the landmark Americans with Disabilities Act. The fund runs a disability rights legal clinic in collaboration with local law schools and provides education, training, and technical assistance to a variety of groups and clients. Established in 1979.

Volunteer Opportunities

DREDF utilizes volunteers as part of a parents' network and as political advocates. Most advocacy volunteers are parents (or other relatives) of children with disabilities with some prior advocacy training or experience. DREDF also uses office volunteers to help with computer and administrative work. A short interview process is required, time commitments are flexible, and training is provided as needed.

Contact Information

Headquarters:
2212 Sixth Street
Berkeley, CA 94710
(510) 644-2555 (V/TTY)
www.dredf.org
dredf@dredf.org

In the summer of 2001, I worked in Yosemite National Park as a volunteer with the Youth Conservation Corps and the Student Conservation Association. I was part of a team responsible for teaching teenagers important lessons on environmental ethics, expedition behavior, and leadership, while at the same time working for the National Park Service on maintenance projects, campground restoration, leech-field construction, and trail work.

Having grown up in Houston and then gone to school in Boston, I knew nothing of the West Coast or Yosemite, and I jumped at the opportunity to spend one summer entirely outdoors. The reality more than met my expectations. Each morning in the backcountry, we would get dressed in jeans and woolen sweaters, search the camp for bear tracks, and head up the trail for breakfast cooked by cheerful, excitable ranger-types. Sitting together on logs, warming our hands with cups of hot chocolate, we would play hearts or write letters or talk about our families. From these quiet mornings and from the work we did, I learned a lot about "firsts," about personal achievement, and about working through stressful, difficult situations. Imagine a tiny but resolute fifteen-year-old girl from New York City chopping wood for the first time, or a seventeen-year-old boy from Connecticut rediscovering a passion for fishing. Now, picture a sixteen-year-old from Atlanta seeing his first mountain, his first forest, his first bear. I also learned the importance of mutual respect, and I realized how enjoyable working for the environment could be. Most importantly, however, every teenager made it home without accident or injury, and with a summer to remember.

—Alan Duke

Indian Law Resource Center

The Indian Law Resource Center works on a range of issues that affect the survival of indigenous communities. Much of their effort focuses on Indian rights to self-government, the recovery and recognition of indigenous lands, the protection and management of natural resources, and the protection of the civil rights of native people. Most recently, the center has extended its outreach to native populations in Central and South America. Established in 1978.

Volunteer Opportunities

The Indian Law Resource Center welcomes volunteers at any time through their Helena, Montana, and Washington, DC offices. Volunteers can assist with fund-raising, help at events, work on the website, and do general administrative work. A short interview is required, and the extent of training depends on the skills of the volunteer and needs of the center.

Contact Information

Michelle Allen
602 North Ewing Street
Helena, MT 59601
(406) 449-2006
　　　or
601 E Street SE
Washington, DC 20003
(202) 547-2800
www.indianlaw.org
mt@indianlaw.org

Mexican American Legal Defense and Educational Fund (MALDEF)

A leader in advocacy for Latino communities, MALDEF's mission is to foster public policy that supports and secures the civil rights of Latinos living in the United States. MALDEF provides community education, collaboration with other organizations, scholarships, and legal advocacy. MALDEF has also worked extensively on redistricting issues and census adjustment. Established in 1968.

Volunteer Opportunities

MALDEF's legal department welcomes law students and clerks to work on specific projects, particularly over the summer months. In the community education and leadership development department, volunteers assist with research. The development department needs help in coordinating special events. MALDEF requests that volunteers commit a minimum of 8 hours a week for at least 2 months. MALDEF asks that volunteers be computer literate and familiar with current software. Interested volunteers should submit a short letter of interest.

Contact Information

634 South Spring Street, Eleventh floor
Los Angeles, CA 90014
(213) 629-2512
www.maldef.org

National Association for the Advancement of Colored People (NAACP)

The NAACP's main goal is to protect and further the civil rights of African Americans and other minority groups. The Washington, DC national office focuses on legislation, advocacy, and political activism, and creates programs and initiatives for its local affiliates. The regional bureaus have several areas of activity, including legal services, education, economic development, a Homeownership and Business Initiative, and a Youth and College Division. To find a local branch near you, check out the NAACP website and click on "Find Us Locally." Established in 1909.

Volunteer Opportunities

The NAACP offers volunteer opportunities at its local affiliates. Specific duties vary between offices, but may include clerical tasks or campaign work.

Contact Information

Headquarters:
NAACP
4805 Mt. Hope Drive
Baltimore, MD 21215
(410) 358-8900
www.naacp.org

National Council of La Raza (NCLR)

Formally affiliated with more than 270 community groups serving 40 states, NCLR assists local Hispanic organizations with resource development, program operations, and management. NCLR also runs the Policy Analysis Center, which researches issues relevant to the Hispanic American community, including education, immigration, housing, health, employment, and civil rights enforcement. Established in 1968.

Volunteer Opportunities

Volunteers assist with the organization of NCLR's annual conference each July. NCLR also welcomes interested individuals to help with membership, marketing, and publicity.

Contact Information

Headquarters:
1111 19th Street NW, Suite 1000
Washington, DC 20036
(202) 785-1670 or (800) 311-NCLR
www.nclr.org

National Urban League

The National Urban League is the nation's oldest and largest community-based movement devoted to the economic and social empowerment of African Americans. Focusing on education and youth, economic self-sufficiency (through good jobs, home ownership, entrepreneurship, and wealth accumulation), and the protection of African American civil rights, the National Urban League works through local offices across the country. Established in 1910.

Volunteer Opportunities

A variety of volunteer opportunities are available at the New York headquarters and at more than 100 affiliate offices across the country.

Contact Information

Headquarters:
120 Wall Street
New York, NY 10005
(212) 558-5300
www.nul.org
info@nul.org

COMMUNITY DEVELOPMENT AND ECONOMIC JUSTICE

AmeriCorps

AmeriCorps, often called the domestic Peace Corps, is a network of hundreds of service programs throughout the United States. AmeriCorps engages more than 40,000 Americans a year in intensive, full-time service projects such as teaching children to read, making neighborhoods safer, building affordable homes, and responding to natural disasters. Many AmeriCorps volunteers work on projects with partner organizations like Habitat for Humanity, the American Red Cross, and Boys and Girls Clubs, as well as other local and national organizations. AmeriCorps members can receive living expenses, health insurance, and education awards to help finance college or pay back student loans. Established in 1993.

Volunteer Opportunities

AmeriCorps is the umbrella organization for three separate programs encompassing more than 1,000 volunteer projects in every state, across a huge range of interests and needs. Volunteers may choose to tutor kids, build housing, restore coastlines, help families in need, clean up rivers and streams, mentor at-risk youth, help seniors live independently, or provide emergency and long-term assistance to victims of natural disasters, to name but a few options. Time commitments vary from 10 months to one year, depending on the project. Most assignments are full-time, but some part-time opportunities are available.

AmeriCorps*NCCC (National Civilian Community Corps) is a 10-month, full-time residential program for volunteers ages 18 to 24. Members work in education, public safety, and the environment, as well as other areas of need.

See also "Volunteers in Service to America (VISTA)" under **Community Development and Economic Justice (p. 29)** and "Corporation for National Service" under **General Resource Organizations (p. 84).**

Contact Information

Corporation for National and Community Service
1201 New York Avenue NW
Washington, DC 20525
(800) 942-2677
http://americorps.org

Association of Community Organizations for Reform Now (ACORN)

Founded by a group of Arkansas welfare mothers, ACORN advocates for the poor and powerless in more than 40 cities across the country. ACORN lobbies and litigates (as well as protests, marches, and employs other direct actions) in five primary areas of concern: schools, jobs, housing, neighborhood safety, and community reinvestment. They have registered more than 500,000 new voters since they were established in 1970.

Volunteer Opportunities

Volunteers are organized through the 41 local offices in 44 cities across the country. Opportunities will vary according to the specific needs of each office, but volunteers are generally used for phone work, administrative duties, petitioning, and transportation.

Contact Information

Headquarters:
88 Third Avenue, Third floor
Brooklyn, NY 11217
(718) 246-7900
www.acorn.org
acornnews@acorn.org

Center for Third World Organizing (CTWO)

CTWO is a training and resource organization dedicated to building a social justice movement led by people of color. CTWO has developed intensive training programs for both new and experienced organizers, including the Movement Activist Apprenticeship Program (MAAP), a 7-week, full-time, field-based internship that teaches the theory and practice of building social justice movements. CTWO also works to establish model multiracial community organizations and to build an active network of organizations and activists of color. With the Applied Research Center, CTWO publishes *ColorLines*, a journal on race, culture, and organizing. Established in 1980.

Volunteer Opportunities

CTWO utilizes volunteers on a case-by-case basis. Volunteers may be asked to work on long-term research projects or help with administrative duties.

Contact Information

1218 East 21st Street
Oakland, CA 94606
(510) 533-7583
www.ctwo.org
ctwo@ctwo.org

Coordinating a literacy-tutoring program at Camp Sweeney, a juvenile detention center for high-school-age boys who are nonviolent offenders, has been a real learning experience for me. My role in the program is to recruit, train, and supervise fifteen tutors who are all UC Berkeley students. I also tutor one student twice a week, helping him to improve his reading and writing skills.

In just a few months, I have learned more about myself than I could have ever hoped to learn in a classroom. Tutoring at Camp Sweeney is different from tutoring students on a college campus or at an elementary school. The young man I tutor wants to learn for his own sake, because he knows that it is important to him. He always comes to tutoring on time. Despite the fact that he has seen so much pain and tragedy in his short life, my tutee has the courage, perseverance, and will to transcend what has been given to him.

Serving at the juvenile detention center has also opened my eyes to a world different from my own, and this experience has strengthened my commitment to the goal of pursuing a career in public policy and civil rights law.

—Tam M. Ma

City Year

City Year is an AmeriCorps program that brings together volunteers ages 17 to 24 from diverse backgrounds for a year of full-time community service. Established in 1988.

Volunteer Opportunities

Volunteers need help too. City Year welcomes adult volunteers to assist AmeriCorps members with their community service, coordinate community service projects, help organize special events, and provide general office assistance.

Contact Information

Headquarters:
285 Columbus Avenue
Boston, MA 02116
(617) 927-2500
www.cityyear.org

Habitat for Humanity

Habitat for Humanity is a nonprofit, faith-based organization built on the notion that every person in need of shelter deserves a decent, affordable home. Habitat sends volunteers to communities throughout the world to construct simple yet livable housing for low-income families. The organization has built more than 100,000 houses in more than 60 countries. Established in 1976.

Volunteer Opportunities

Habitat for Humanity affiliates across the country offer opportunities to participate in the building of a Habitat home in your area. Habitat welcomes individuals, large groups, and people of all ages. Habitat's WomenBuild program organizes building projects solely for female volunteers. Volunteers who work at Habitat's headquarters or in local offices may receive living stipends and housing and health benefits.

Contact Information

Headquarters:
121 Habitat Street
Americus, GA 31709-3498
(229) 924-6935
www.habitat.org

National Association of Community Action Agencies (NACAA)

NACAA represents the interests of more than 1,000 community action agencies across the country. Community action agencies are nonprofit private and public organizations established under the Economic Opportunity Act of 1964 to fight poverty at the local level. NACAA publishes a journal, a monthly newsletter, and biweekly reports addressing the needs of community action agencies. They also conduct and publish surveys, hold an annual policy forum, and sponsor an annual National Community Action Month as well as the National Dialogue on Poverty conference every four years. Established in 1972.

Volunteer Opportunities

Volunteers are needed throughout the year for administrative assistance and for help from mid-August through September in preparing for NACAA's annual conference.

Contact Information

Community Action Partnership
1100 17th Street NW, Suite 500
Washington, DC 20036
(202) 265-7546
www.nacaa.org
info@nacaa.org

Neighbor to Neighbor (N2N)

Neighbor to Neighbor provides permanent affordable housing, special-needs housing, and other housing services to low- and middle-income families in Colorado.

Volunteer Opportunities

Neighbor to Neighbor welcomes volunteers in Colorado to assist in a variety of capacities, including administrative work, child care, landscape and property maintenance, building fences and playgrounds, painting, cleaning, weeding and pruning, teaching workshops, grant writing, marketing, and volunteer counseling. N2N is happy to tailor projects to the specific skills of volunteers. Established in 1970.

Contact Information

424 Pine Street, Suite #203
Fort Collins, CO 80524
(970) 484-7498
www.n2n.org

Oxfam America

Oxfam America provides support to local groups dealing with the issues of poverty, hunger, and social injustice around the globe. A privately funded organization that is based on the Oxford Committee for Famine Relief, which originated in Great Britain in 1942, Oxfam America advocates among national and international policy makers for humane public policies that address the underlying impediments to ending poverty and hunger. Oxfam also supports emergency relief efforts—supplying vital resources such as food, water, shelter, and clothing—in areas where natural disasters and humanitarian crises affect its partner communities. There are eleven independent Oxfam organizations worldwide, loosely joined in a confederation, Oxfam International. Established in 1970.

Volunteer Opportunities

Oxfam America offers many volunteer opportunities through their Boston headquarters and Washington, DC advocacy office. Additionally, there are often seasonal opportunities involving special events in other parts of the United States. Oxfam America welcomes volunteers' technical skills and time to support program work, raise funds, and educate the public. They can often tailor volunteer opportunities to fit specific interests, skills, and available time.

Contact Information

Headquarters:
26 West Street
Boston, MA 02111
(800) 77-OXFAM, (617) 482-1211
        or
1112 16th Street NW, Suite 600
Washington, DC 20036
(202) 496-1180
www.oxfamamerica.org
helpinghand@oxfamamerica.org

Project America

Project America creates community service projects for corporations and large member organizations. Established in 1993.

Volunteer Opportunities

Project America creates custom service projects for large groups. In the past, Project America has hosted an annual day of service for the entire country and Alternative Spring Break, which invites college students to participate in community service during their spring vacations.

Contact Information

1520 West Main Street, Suite 102
Richmond, VA 23220
(804) 358-1605
http://project.org

United Students Against Sweatshops (USAS)

USAS is a coalition of more than 200 international university groups working to end sweatshop labor conditions and support workers' rights around the world. Established in 1998.

Volunteer Opportunities

USAS volunteers work through chapter affiliates at universities across the country and internationally.

Contact Information

Headquarters:
888 16th Street NW, Suite 303
Washington, DC 20006
(202) NO-SWEAT
www.usasnet.org

The Urban Coalition

The Urban Coalition is a research and advocacy organization working to empower low-income and minority communities and to improve their access to education, health care, and employment. Established in 1967.

Volunteer Opportunities

Volunteers in the St. Paul area can work with the Urban Coalition on research, education, and outreach projects, including data analysis, community outreach, interviewing, and administrative tasks.

Contact Information

2610 University Avenue West, Suite 201
St. Paul, MN 55114
(612) 348-8550
www.urbancoalition.org
gen@urbancoalition.org

Volunteers in Service to America (Americorps*VISTA)

VISTA members have served in poor communities for more than 35 years, working to fight illiteracy, improve health services, create businesses, increase housing opportunities, and bridge the digital divide. Now in partnership with AmeriCorps, AmeriCorps*VISTA supports nearly 6,000 full-time volunteers, working and living in the communities they serve. Established in 1964.

Volunteer Opportunities

VISTA volunteers are assigned for one year, full time, to a nonprofit organization working in an underserved community. Responsibilities might include recruiting and training volunteers, fund-raising and grant writing, eliciting corporate sponsorship and donations, planning community meetings, and handling public relations. Volunteers must be at least 18 years old. Many programs seek volunteers with college degrees or at least three years of work experience. Initiative, flexibility, and organizational skills are a must. Fluency in Spanish or other languages is helpful in certain programs. Volunteers are given a living allowance, health insurance, and relocation expenses (if needed), as well as an education award of $4,725 which can be used to help pay for college, graduate school, or vocational training, or to pay off student loans (a $1,200 stipend can be substituted). Child-care assistance is available.

See also "AmeriCorps" under **Community Development and Economic Justice** (p. 22) and "Corporation for National Service" under **General Resource Organizations** (p. 84).

Contact Information

Corporation for National and Community Service
1201 New York Avenue NW
Washington, DC 20525
(800) 942-2677
http://americorps.org/vista

Volunteers of America

Volunteers of America is a national spiritually based organization that provides volunteer opportunities and service programs on a local level in communities across the country. Volunteers of America is one of the nation's largest nonprofit providers of quality affordable housing for families, the elderly, and people with disabilities. They are also a provider of skilled long-term nursing care and health services, operating nursing facilities, residential assisted-living complexes, and retirement communities. Established in 1896.

Volunteer Opportunities

Opportunities abound on a local level. Volunteers of America works in the following areas: youth services, community enhancement, correctional services, developmentally disabled services, elderly services, emergency services, employment and training services, health-care services, homeless services, housing services, mental health, and substance abuse.

Contact Information

Headquarters:
1660 Duke Street
Alexandria, VA 22314-3421
(800) 899-0089 or (703) 341-5000
www.volunteersofamerica.org

In the spring of 1964, I was a politically awakened undergraduate at a private college (Williams) in New England. Though from a privileged background, I had become familiar with the persistence of poverty through my teenage experiences working with migrant farmworkers on my uncle's farm. Thus, I was intrigued when I read about a summer project in eastern Kentucky. College students would be living with coal-mining families while working to build a network of community-based organizations. The idea was to involve local people, as opposed to courthouse politicians, in John F. Kennedy's Appalachian Redevelopment Program, a forerunner of Lyndon Johnson's War on Poverty.

The months I spent in Kentucky were a truly formative experience. I began to see the world through different eyes and came back not only dedicated to community work but feeling very much at ease around people from all different kinds of backgrounds. In a sense, I found not only a way to be in the world but the real meaning of citizenship—defining myself in terms of my commitment to the betterment of the numerous communities where I have lived and worked over the years.

—Peter Booth Wiley

EDUCATION

Educators for Social Responsibility (ESR)

ESR provides educators with programs and resources that emphasize emotional learning, character education, conflict resolution, violence prevention, and intergroup relations. Their largest program, the Resolving Conflict Creatively Program (RCCP), is a comprehensive K-12 school-based program that provides a model for preventing violence in the schools. RCCP has been implemented in more than 375 schools in the United States. Established in 1984.

Volunteer Opportunities

ESR welcomes volunteers to help in their office with administrative duties and mailings. Time commitments are flexible and training is provided.

Contact Information

23 Garden Street
Cambridge, MA 02138
(800) 370-2515 or (617) 492-1764
www.esrnational.org
educators@esrnational.org

Literacy Volunteers of America, Inc. (LVA)

LVA is a national organization devoted to promoting adult literacy through its local affiliates. Through its national tutoring program, LVA helps adults learn to read, write, and speak English proficiently. LVA also creates and publicizes campaigns for public advocacy about literacy. Established in 1962.

Volunteer Opportunities

LVA offers positions in tutoring (training is provided), fund-raising, special events coordination, publicity, administrative support, and board service.

Contact Information

Headquarters:
635 James Street
Syracuse, NY 13203-2214
(315) 472-0001
www.literacyvolunteers.org

From 1994 to 1996, I served with two different AmeriCorps programs in the Bronx, New York. I weatherized low-income housing, helped educate families on the dangers of lead poisoning, and built gardens in vacant lots with neighborhood kids. I returned to the same neighborhoods for a second service year to work with a job-skills program for young adults (ages eighteen to twenty-two) who had never completed high school. I taught GED preparation classes, counseled students on their higher education opportunities, and coordinated a speakers series on different career paths, life skills, and the exploration of race and culture in urban communities.

This was the first time I had been surrounded by other people who, like me, want to understand and rebuild communities. During my time in the Bronx, I learned from priests, policemen, high school kids, homeless families, and longtime community activists. I walked the halls of urban schools, public housing projects, local churches, and community centers. I learned the history of urban America through the eyes of people who contribute to their communities daily. I also learned how to be a community member. Now I find myself naturally finding time to tutor neighborhood kids, to join community planning meetings, and to advocate for the rights of families and children in my neighborhood.

—Chandra Egan

Publicolor

Publicolor cleans up, brightens, revitalizes, and transforms neglected public spaces in New York City, particularly those used by inner-city youth.

Volunteer Opportunities

Publicolor paints schools and other public buildings in New York City every Saturday from 10:30 a.m. to 2:30 p.m. Volunteers are matched with students for the day. Students teach volunteers how to paint; volunteers share school, work, and life experiences with the students to create short-term, mutual mentoring relationships. Publicolor welcomes corporate, service, and school groups, as well as interested individuals. Established in 1996.

Contact Information

114 East 32nd Street, Suite 900
New York, NY 10016
(212) 213-6121
www.publicolor.org
volunteers@publicolor.org

Teach for America

Teach for America trains recent college graduates to become educators in low-income public schools throughout the country, in both rural and urban settings. The mission of Teach for America is to bring motivated teachers to underprivileged classrooms and to equip college graduates with the skills they need to become leaders in the educational community and beyond. Established in 1989.

Volunteer Opportunities

Teach for America teachers must attend a five-week summer training course in either New York City or Houston, and must commit to 2 years of service. Teachers typically earn between $22,000 and $40,000 per year. Visit the website to locate a regional office or to download an application.

Contact information

315 West 36th Street, Sixth floor
New York, NY 10018
(800) 832-1230 ext. 2
www.teachforamerica.org

ENVIRONMENT AND SUSTAINABLE COMMUNITIES

American Rivers

American Rivers is a national conservation organization dedicated to preserving and restoring America's rivers while promoting awareness about the importance of healthy waterways in the natural environment and in our communities. American Rivers' programs also focus on dam removal, flood control, hydropower policy reform, endangered species protection, water quality, and reviving neighborhood rivers. Established in 1973.

Volunteer Opportunities

American Rivers has limited volunteer opportunities through their Washington, DC headquarters. Full-time or near full-time internships are available for students and recent college graduates for work on a variety of conservation issues. Internships range from 3 to 6 months. More flexible volunteer commitments may be available in field offices located in South Dakota, Tennessee, Oregon, Washington, Connecticut, Nebraska, Montana, Pennsylvania, Iowa, and California.

Contact Information

Headquarters:
1025 Vermont Avenue NW, Suite 720
Washington, DC 20005
(202) 347-7550
www.americanrivers.org

Center for Environmental Citizenship (CEC)

CEC was created by campus activists to encourage college students to be environmentally aware and active. CEC educates, trains, and organizes young people to be advocates for the environment. Established in 1992.

Volunteer Opportunities

The Washington, DC office holds Tuesday volunteer nights, from 5:00 to 8:00 p.m.

Contact Information

Headquarters:
200 G Street NE, Suite 300
Washington, DC 20002
www.envirocitizen.org
cec@envirocitizen.org

Center for Health, Environment, and Justice (CHEJ)

Lois Gibbs, a community leader at Love Canal, began CHEJ as the Citizens Clearinghouse for Hazardous Waste in 1981, based on the principle that everyone has the right to a clean and healthy environment. Fundamentally taking a grass-roots approach, CHEJ provides information, technical assistance, and know-how to local citizens and organizations fighting to hold industry and government accountable in their communities. Established in 1981.

Volunteer Opportunities

Volunteers can assist with general office work and research.

Contact Information

150 South Washington Street, Suite 300
P.O. Box 6806
Falls Church, VA 22040
(703) 237-2249
www.chej.org
chej@chej.org

Council for Responsible Genetics (CRG)

CRG, an organization of scientists, environmentalists, public health advocates, physicians, lawyers, and other concerned citizens, encourages informed public debate about the social, ethical, and environmental implications of new genetic technologies and advocates for socially responsible use of these technologies. CRG is currently tracking biotechnology developments, writing position papers, creating model legislation, providing public education, and alerting the public to issues in a variety of areas including: cloning, biopiracy, biosafety, germline engineering, genetically modified foods, genetic privacy and discrimination, DNA databanking, life patents, and xenotransplantation. In addition, CRG publishes a bimonthly magazine, *GeneWatch*, that monitors the ethical, social, and ecological impacts of biotechnology. Established in 1983.

Volunteer Opportunities

CRG generally uses graduate students with scientific backgrounds in project-based internships. Others with advanced skills should contact the office for information. Additionally, volunteers can assist in the office with administrative duties.

Contact Information

5 Upland Road, Suite 3
Cambridge, MA 02140
(617) 868-0870
www.gene-watch.org
crg@gene-watch.org

Earth Island Institute (EII)

EII offers organizational support to a host of environmentalist groups working on more than 30 projects worldwide: protecting rain forests, marine mammals, sea turtles, and indigenous lands; promoting organic and sustainable agriculture, ecological paper alternatives, and the emerging Russian environmental movement; and pursuing community-based habitat restoration, reduction of marine pollution, and the development of urban multicultural environmental leadership. Established in 1982.

Volunteer Opportunities

Earth Island Network Services, the umbrella organization, welcomes volunteers to help with special events, administrative duties, and mailings in their San Francisco office. Additionally, many of the projects affiliated with Earth Island Institute use volunteers for a wide variety of tasks. Many of these projects and their contact numbers are listed below, but also visit the EII website for current opportunities.

Baikal Watch needs volunteers who can do web and other research on a variety of topics. They are particularly interested in people with

Russian, Mongolian, or Chinese language fluency. (415) 788-3666 ext. 109

Bluewater Network is seeking general office help and research assistants for either short- or long-term projects, with a one-month minimum time commitment. (415) 788-3666 ext. 150

Center for Safe Energy seeks highly motivated people with computer know-how for short- and long-term projects. (510) 883-1177

Earthinfo.org needs interns and volunteers to do research for a cutting-edge environmental website. Work from home or from their San Francisco office. (415) 788-3666 ext. 238

Global Service Corps welcomes prospective volunteers with resumes in hand. (415) 788-3666 ext. 128

ReThink Paper offers internships in Portland and San Francisco. Volunteers may assist with campaign organizing, publications, environmental education, website development, research, networking/coalition building, fund-raising, and administrative support. Self-motivated individuals are preferred, and computer savvy is helpful but not critical. (415) 788-3666 ext. 232

Sacred Land Film Project is seeking volunteers with computer and clerical skills for short-term projects. A car is necessary, and volunteers should be open to coming to La Honda, California, about one day per week. (650) 747-0685

Tibetan Plateau Project is seeking volunteers to assist with research, writing, fund-raising, and administrative tasks. (415) 788-3666 ext. 132

Contact Information

EII Headquarters:
300 Broadway, Suite 28
San Francisco, CA 94133
(415) 788-3666
www.earthisland.org
earthisland@earthisland.org

Friends of the Earth (FOE)

With affiliates in 63 countries, FOE supports individuals and organizations who are working to ensure a healthy environment in their communities.

FOE monitors U.S. and international policies on the environment, and sponsors the Safer Food, Safer Farms Campaign and the Healing the Atmosphere Campaign. Established in 1969.

Volunteer Opportunities

FOE offers volunteer opportunities as projects arise. Duties may include administrative assistance, as well as help in preparing for demonstrations and marches.

Contact Information

1025 Vermont Avenue NW
Washington, DC 20005
(202) 783-7400 ext. 241
www.foe.org

In my senior year of college at Tufts University, I volunteered with Arts in Progress, a nonprofit arts organization in Boston, and worked as a teaching assistant for grades K-5 at a bilingual elementary school in Jamaica Plains. In this position, I created art curriculum, taught classes, and worked one-on-one with students. This experience strengthened my belief in the value of art education. The students were full of energy and uninhibited in their creative exploration. Art class was a time in their day when they could be playful and express themselves through words, paint, and imagery. The use of art in the classroom led to discussions about identity, home, and family, and it also taught students about formal aesthetics and visual concepts. I also learned about the benefits and frustrations of bilingual education and working in the public school system.

Volunteering has helped me focus my own goals and interests. This year I am working as a volunteer at Southern Exposure, a nonprofit arts organization and gallery in San Francisco's Mission district that exhibits emerging artists and also coordinates art programming in public schools. I think it is important to have a positive impact on one's community, and for me, working with children and art is both rewarding and a lot of fun.

—Amanda Bornstein

Greenpeace

Greenpeace uses direct actions and "creative communications" to protect the global environment. More than 2.5 million members worldwide support their efforts to preserve ancient forests and oceans, put an end to global warming, eliminate pollutants in the environment, eliminate genetic engineering of our food supply, and promote nuclear disarmament. Established in 1971.

Volunteer Opportunities

Greenpeace offers internship opportunities at their headquarters in Washington, DC. The intern program gives students experience with a range of departments within the Greenpeace organization.

Contact Information

U.S. Headquarters:
702 H Street NW, Suite 300
Washington, DC 20001
(800) 326-0959
www.greenpeaceusa.org
greenpeaceusa@wdc.greenpeace.org

The Nature Conservancy

The Nature Conservancy works with communities and businesses to protect lands and waters around the world. Established in 1951.

Volunteer Opportunities

Volunteer opportunities vary from chapter to chapter, and may involve working on land preserves (including habitat restoration, planting trees, building fences, and maintaining trails), and helping with land monitoring. Some chapters train volunteers to give slide shows or presentations in their communities.

Contact Information

Headquarters:
4245 North Fairfax Drive, Suite 100
Arlington, VA 22203
(800) 628-6860
http://nature.org
comment@tnc.org

Pesticide Action Network North America (PANNA)

PANNA links more than 100 health, consumer, labor, environmental, progressive agriculture, and public interest groups in a global network to fight the use and proliferation of pesticides. PANNA analyzes the environmental and public health impacts of pesticides and genetically engineered crops, investigates the role of corporations and governments in the use and promotion of pesticides and genetically engineered crops, and works to reduce reliance on pesticides and engineered crops by promoting sustainable agriculture. Established in 1982.

Volunteer Opportunities

Volunteers work with staff on a variety of activities, from research and outreach for specific campaigns to staffing tables at community events. Besides becoming informed on pesticide-related issues, volunteers gain experience in the day-to-day operation of a non-governmental organization and learn how advocacy, coalition building, and organizational development are conducted. PANNA seeks volunteers who share a commitment to environmental and social justice issues and a special interest in pesticide reform. Interested people should be self-motivated, capable of working independently, and willing to work flexibly in a team. Good communication and computer skills are desired, and additional language skills are a plus. For full-time volunteers, PANNA provides a small stipend to cover transportation costs.

Contact Information

Susan Kegley
49 Powell Street, Suite 500
San Francisco, CA 94102
(415) 981-1771
www.panna.org
skegley@panna.org

Project Underground

Project Underground works to expose and combat problems created by the mining and oil industries. To that end, they provide informational, technical, legal, and scientific support to communities near oil, gas, and mining operations. Project Underground assists community groups by networking them with other communities, mounting legal challenges, creating publicity, and organizing nonviolent, strategic campaigning tactics. Established in 1996.

Volunteer Opportunities

Volunteers are welcome to assist with research, administration, and campaign-related tasks, including organizing conferences and meetings, fundraising, and producing special events. Project Underground offers extended volunteer opportunities in the summer, when individuals can work intensely on specific campaigns. Training is provided as needed.

Contact Information

1916A Martin Luther King Jr. Way
Berkeley, CA 94704
(510) 705-8981
www.moles.org
project_underground@moles.org

I am originally from Houston, Texas. I began community service in junior high when I visited retirement homes and spent time with the elderly. I also became very involved with Kick Drugs Out of America, an organization founded by Chuck Norris and supported by many prominent people, including the Bush family, that goes to inner-city public schools and teaches martial arts to students. The program also helps with self-esteem and discipline, and it stresses drug prevention among teenagers. In high school I visited foster homes and spent time with abandoned children. I also went to Mexico on occasion to build houses for families. At college I wanted to continue spending time with organizations that deal with people—specifically the elderly and children. I volunteered for the Big Brothers Big Sisters organization, Cal-Corps, and the North Berkeley Senior Center.

It has been terrific to volunteer with organizations that I really believe in. It has been so fulfilling to give my time to people who are less fortunate than I am. I love meeting new people and giving them a helping hand in life. I feel that one has to give in order to receive. I have also learned that it takes people getting involved and taking real action for our communities, as well as our world, to become better places.

—Darol Ryan

Rainforest Action Network (RAN)

RAN works to raise public awareness of the condition of rain forests through education and direct action. RAN works in conjunction with the international rain-forest conservation movement by supporting activists in rain-forest countries and organizing consumers and community action groups in the United States. RAN has developed a 500-year plan to halt deforestation and address global forest protection, certified logging, diversifying the fiber supply (such as tree-free paper), reducing consumption, and transforming government and corporate policies. Established in 1985.

Volunteer Opportunities

Volunteers are needed for general office work, data entry, mailings, and making banners and signs in RAN's San Francisco office, weekdays from 9:00 a.m. to 5:30 p.m. RAN holds bulk-mail pizza parties on Thursday evenings from 6:00 to 10:00 p.m. at which volunteers prepare educational and membership materials for mailing. Specialty volunteer opportunities are occasionally available in graphic arts, demonstration support, photography, horticulture, translation, and other areas.

Contact Information

Adrienne Blum
221 Pine Street, Suite 500
San Francisco, CA 94104
(415) 398-4404
www.ran.org
helpran@ran.org

Sierra Club

Begun by John Muir in 1892, the Sierra Club's first conservation campaign was to block a proposed reduction of Yosemite National Park. Today the Sierra Club has more than 700,000 members and is one of the nation's largest and oldest grass-roots conservation organizations. Their mission: explore, enjoy, and protect the wild places of the earth; practice and promote the responsible use of the earth's ecosystems and resources; and educate and enlist humanity to protect and restore the quality of the natural and human environment. Established in 1892.

Volunteer Opportunities

Sierra Club utilizes and provides extensive training to volunteers at every level of involvement, from national leadership to regional committees, neighborhood canvassing, and office support. Volunteers might lead hikes or write letters, advocate for specific legislation, attend council meetings, lobby local and state legislators, canvas in support of candidates and issues, work phone banks, and stuff envelopes, to name but a few possibilities. Volunteers are organized through local chapters.

Contact Information

Headquarters:
85 Second Street, Second floor
San Francisco, CA 94105-3441
(415) 977-5500
www.sierraclub.org
information@sierraclub.org

Trust for Public Land (TPL)

TPL's legal and real-estate specialists work with government and community groups to preserve natural and historic spaces for human enjoyment. Established in 1972.

Volunteer Opportunities

Volunteers are organized through regional offices and are utilized on a per-project basis. Activities may include planting trees, working in community gardens, and cleaning up parks and other spaces, as well as community research and outreach.

Contact Information

116 New Montgomery Street, Fourth floor
San Francisco, CA 94105
(415) 495-4014
www.tpl.org

Willing Workers on Organic Farms (WWOOF)

WWOOF is an international membership organization which matches people interested in volunteering on organic farms with host farms. Established in 1971.

Volunteer Opportunities

WWOOF provides interested individuals with listings of volunteer opportunities on organic farms in the United States and around the world.

Volunteers must become members of WWOOF to participate. Responsibilities will vary, but may include activities such as sowing, making compost, gardening, cutting wood, weeding, harvesting, building, milking, feeding animals, and other activities that help small farms operate.

Contact Information

WWOOF USA:
4429 Carlson Road
Nelson, British Columbia
Canada V1L 6X3
(250) 354-4417
www.wwoofusa.com
wwoofcan@uniserve.com

My year-long community service stint was a nine-hundred-hour commitment to the Alameda County Collaborative on Resource Development for Youth. The forty-member team provided resources to the community for service-learning, environmental education, volunteer recruitment, creative reuse of "waste," and partnership building. My specific assignment was to coordinate volunteers for an after-school homework program. After the school year ended, I was reassigned to be a counselor at the East Oakland Boxing Association and Recreation Center. I had a great time and loads of fun.

During my service, I learned a plethora of skills to help my community. But more importantly, I learned about my role there and about the community itself. I became an active citizen. My efforts became my reward. I was ecstatic to learn about so many jobs and to meet so many concerned individuals who wanted to address the needs of the community rather than seek personal success. Together, we gave our time and energy, and in return we received the gift of friendship, from each other and the community. I developed a social conscience that was built on responsibility, not guilt. Community service did not show me how to live; it just showed me what life is like as a dynamic participant.

—Ryan Sim

FREE SPEECH AND GOVERNMENT ACCOUNTABILITY

Common Cause

Common Cause works for open, accountable government and the right of all citizens to be involved in shaping our nation's public policies. Common Cause does not accept foundation or government grants or solicit contributions from labor unions or corporations. High-priority national issues include campaign finance reform, civil rights, and ethics in government. Established in 1970.

Volunteer Opportunities

Common Cause welcomes short- and long-term volunteers in both their national and state offices. In the national office, volunteers inform and activate Common Cause membership, track issues in the press, monitor congressional committee meetings, respond to inquiries about the organization and its legislative efforts, and serve as administrative aides. In state offices, volunteers lobby lawmakers on reform issues and work at the grass roots to educate voters and rally citizen support for Common Cause issues. Volunteers work closely with staff members, who provide them with background materials and organize seminars on Common Cause issues and the skills of political advocacy.

Contact Information

Headquarters:
1250 Connecticut Avenue NW
Washington, DC 20036
(202) 736-5705
www.commoncause.org

National Coalition Against Censorship (NCAC)

NCAC supports public access to information and opposes restrictions on free expression. An alliance of 50 literary, artistic, religious, educational, professional, labor, and civil liberties groups, NCAC works to educate its member organizations and the public about the dangers of censorship and how to fight against it. Established in 1974.

Volunteer Opportunities

NCAC welcomes volunteers for administrative work and outreach in their New York office. Individuals outside of New York who wish to participate in NCAC causes should visit their website for local opportunities.

Contact Information

275 Seventh Avenue, Ninth floor
New York, NY 10001
(212) 807-6222
www.ncac.org
ncac@ncac.org

National Voting Rights Institute (NVRI)

NVRI is a legal advocacy center that aims to redefine the campaign-finance-reform debate as a voting-rights issue. To that end, they have launched a series of court challenges to counter unlimited campaign spending, and they advocate for the use of public funds for campaign finance as a way to even the playing field for low- and moderate-income candidates. Established in 1994.

Volunteer Opportunities

NVRI welcomes volunteers to help with administrative duties in their Boston office. Time commitments are flexible, and training is provided.

Contact Information

One Bromfield Street, Third floor
Boston, MA 02108
(617) 368-9100
www.nvri.org
nvri@nvri.org

People for the American Way (PFAW) and PFAW Foundation

PFAW works to combat intolerance, promote public involvement in the democratic process, and defend constitutional rights. Areas of activism include: ensuring quality public education, monitoring the religious right, and fighting censorship in the arts, literature, speech, and cyberspace. Established in 1980.

Volunteer Opportunities

PFAW holds weekly meetings at their Washington, DC office. Activities include phone banking, preparing mailings, data entry, and canvassing and election work. For meeting times and places, contact the Capital Volunteer Coordinator at (202) 467-4999. Visit PFAW's website for volunteer opportunities in other areas.

Contact Information

2000 M Street NW, Suite 400
Washington, DC 20036
(800) 326-7329
www.pfaw.org

Project Vote

Project Vote is a nonpartisan organization working to register voters and increase election turnout in low-income and minority communities. Since its creation in 1982, Project Vote has registered 2.7 million new voters. Project Vote does not endorse any candidates or parties. Established in 1982.

Volunteer Opportunities

Volunteers are needed each year from late summer through fall to help register voters and get out the vote. Volunteers might staff tables, go door-to-door, hand out literature, make phone calls, or work on election day. Time commitments are flexible, and some training is provided. Project Vote targets elections in different communities from year to year.

Contact Information

Headquarters:
88 Third Avenue, Third floor
Brooklyn, NY 11217
(718) 246-7929
www.projectvote.org

I became a VISTA volunteer near my thirtieth birthday, much older than my partners in service. Nonetheless, my enthusiasm enabled me to make the two-thousand-mile move and live on a small stipend. After living all my life in Michigan, I was placed in Peres Elementary School in Richmond, California, as a tutor coordinator.

During my shy, awkward childhood, I excelled in some areas, but I struggled in my reading, often having trouble focusing and comprehending words on the page. After attaining a B.A. in English from Central Michigan University and becoming an avid reader, I felt I had overcome a reading disorder. Knowing that I could do it committed me to the notion that all kids can learn to read and enjoy it.

It's difficult to sum up all the learning, growth, touching moments, and frustrations that occurred during my two years in VISTA. I don't want to oversentimentalize the experience. It was rough. There were never enough tutors. Our program had financial struggles. I had financial nightmares! On occasion, I had to turn down coffee with friends to save money for public transportation. However, I learned how to survive on very little while realizing that there are families who survive on even less. Most significantly, I witnessed great moments of rapport between kids and tutors. I am proud to say that after my term with VISTA expired, I became a full-time tutor coordinator at Peres.

—Dave Cowen

Public Citizen

Public Citizen was founded by Ralph Nader to represent the consumer public against special-interest and corporate lobbyists. Public Citizen has worked for openness and accountability in government, fair trade policies, affordable prescription drugs and health care, alternative energy sources, and a healthy environment, among other progressive issues. Established in 1971.

Volunteer Opportunities

Public Citizen welcomes volunteers in their Washington, DC office. Volunteers may assist with research, publications, and administrative responsibilities.

Contact Information

1600 20th Street NW
Washington, DC 20009
(202) 588-1000
www.citizen.org
pcmail@citizen.org

The Ruckus Society

The Ruckus Society provides nonviolent civil disobedience training and support for environmental and human rights activists and organizations. Established in 1995.

Volunteer Opportunities

The Ruckus Society offers a variety of part- and full-time internships and volunteer opportunities on a quarterly basis through their office in Oakland, California. Volunteers interested in long-term projects are required to submit a resume and two-page project proposal and must commit to a minimum of 10 hours a week for 2 to 3 months. Short-term or one-time volunteer opportunities are available on a rotating basis.

Contact Information

4131 Shafter Avenue, Suite 9
Oakland, CA 94609
(510) 595-3442
www.ruckus.org
info@ruckus.org

GAY AND LESBIAN RIGHTS

Gay, Lesbian, and Straight Education Network (GLSEN)

GLSEN works with teachers, administrators, and other adults in the schools, and with policy makers at all levels, to combat homophobia in the education system. GLSEN promotes gay-straight alliances, publishes *Respect* magazine, trains staff, and works against student and teacher discrimination and harassment. Through an information-heavy website, GLSEN also keeps the public informed on subjects such as the Boy Scouts of America's anti-gay policies and related local school board issues. Established in 1993.

Volunteer Opportunities

Volunteers are organized through local chapters in more than 40 states.

Contact Information

121 West 27th Street, Suite 804
New York, NY 10001
(212) 727-0135
www.glsen.org
glsen@glsen.org

International Gay and Lesbian Human Rights Commission (IGLHRC)

IGLHRC monitors and mobilizes responses to human rights abuses against lesbians, gay men, bisexuals, transgendered people, and people with HIV and AIDS worldwide. Established in 1991.

Volunteer Opportunities

IGLHRC welcomes volunteers for a variety of tasks, including translating materials; doing research and database entry; reading periodicals for news items; helping with fund-raising efforts; and preparing mailings to activists, attorneys, and supporters. IGLHRC also holds weekly volunteer nights at their San Francisco office. Commitments can be flexible, but most volunteers devote 2 to 4 hours weekly.

Contact Information

1360 Mission Street, Suite 200
San Francisco, CA 94103
(415) 255-8680
www.iglhrc.org
iglhrc@iglhrc.org

National Gay and Lesbian Task Force (NGLTF)

In 1973, NGLTF successfully campaigned to eliminate the American Psychiatric Association's classification of homosexuality as a mental illness. Today, NGLTF continues to protect and encourage the civil rights of gay, lesbian, bisexual, and transgendered people through coalition building, research, critical policy analysis, strategy development, public education, and legal and legislative challenges. Established in 1973.

Volunteer Opportunities

NGLTF has a drop-in volunteer night every Thursday evening from 7:00 to 9:00 p.m. at the NGLTF offices in Washington, DC. NGLTF is also seeking a group of volunteers to assist with NGLTF events in the DC area. Activities include phone banking on state and local issues, staffing tables at local events, participating in events representing NGLTF, and assisting with local fund-raising projects.

Contact Information

1700 Kalorama Road NW
Washington, DC 20009-2624
(202) 332-6483
www.ngltf.org

HEALTH CARE, HUNGER, AND HOMELESSNESS

AIDS Coalition to Unleash Power (ACT UP)

ACT UP began in New York City in 1987 as an organization "united in anger and committed to direct action to end the AIDS crisis." ACT UP has been instrumental on many fronts in the fight against AIDS. Through campaigns of direct action they have educated students about condom use, distributed clean needles to intravenous drug users, successfully lobbied the Food and Drug Administration for the early release of experimental AIDS treatments, and worked to lower the prices of pharmaceuticals. Established in 1987.

Volunteer Opportunities

General ACT UP meetings are held in Manhattan every Monday at 7:30 p.m. at the Lesbian, Gay, Bisexual, and Transgendered Community Center, 208 West 13th Street. Meetings are open, everyone is welcome, opportunities for activism abound.

Contact Information

332 Bleecker Street, Suite G5
New York, NY 10014
(212) 966-4873
www.actupny.org
actupny@panix.com

America's Second Harvest

America's Second Harvest serves more than 26 million people each year, distributing donated food to food banks and food-rescue programs across America. Established in 1979.

Volunteer Opportunities

America's Second Harvest encourages interested individuals to volunteer locally at food banks in their community.

Contact Information

35 East Wacker Drive, #2000
Chicago, IL 60601
(800) 771-2303
www.secondharvest.org

After growing up in a variety of communities, including a small town in northern New Mexico and a poor neighborhood in urban Minneapolis, I decided to attend a small liberal arts college in Portland, Oregon. Even though I looked like most of my peers, I had a hard time relating to their life experiences. I started to volunteer as a literacy tutor for homeless men, mostly because I wanted an excuse to go into neighborhoods that felt more like home than my college campus. I got involved in homeless advocacy and other social issues. Other students started to ask me how to get involved in similar ways. It was then that I realized that college students needed ways to learn about community problems in real-life settings, so I started a community service office on my campus to encourage students to get more involved in confronting social problems. When I graduated from college, that office had two professional staff members and ran over twenty different programs.

Involvement in community service and working for social justice have allowed me to become part of many incredible communities. I have learned a lot about myself, and my life feels more meaningful because I know that I can contribute to resolving some of our social problems.

—Megan Voorhees

Bread for the World

Bread for the World mobilizes citizens to support policies that address the root causes of hunger and poverty. Thousands of local churches and community groups make up Bread for the World's network of activists involved in letter-writing campaigns, telephone trees, and action campaigns. Bread for the World's partner organization, Bread for the World Institute, carries out research and education on hunger, and also publishes an annual hunger report. Established in 1972.

Volunteer Opportunities

Volunteers can organize letter-writing campaigns, create telephone trees to call members of Congress, and participate in media activism, study groups, and educational outreach in their communities.

Contact Information

Headquarters:
50 F Street NW, Suite 500
Washington, DC 20001
(800) 82-BREAD or (202) 639-9400
www.bread.org

Daily Bread

Daily Bread is a grass-roots, all-volunteer organization which distributes food in Berkeley and Oakland, California. Established in 1983.

Volunteer Opportunities

Volunteers are assigned a weekly run to pick up and deliver donated food. Volunteers must have a car and must commit to approximately one hour per week.

Contact Information

2447 Prince Street
Oakland, CA 94705
(510) 848-3522

Elizabeth Glaser Pediatric AIDS Foundation

The foundation is the leading nonprofit organization in the nation that funds and conducts research on the pediatric aspects of AIDS and other life-threatening diseases. Established in 1988.

Volunteer Opportunities

The Elizabeth Glaser Pediatric AIDS Foundation needs volunteers to assist with administrative duties at their offices in Santa Monica, New York City, and Washington, DC.

Contact Information

Headquarters:
2950 31st Street, #125
Santa Monica, CA 90405
(310) 314-1459 (Santa Monica)
(212) 448-6654 (New York)
(202) 296-9165 (Washington, DC)
www.pedaids.org
info@pedaids.org

Food First

Food First was founded in the wake of the success of the book *Diet For a Small Planet* and is dedicated to the notion that access to food is a basic human right. Also known as the Institute for Food and Development Policy, Food First researches the causes of hunger and poverty and works toward "value-based solutions" through education, outreach, and analysis. Established in 1975.

Volunteer Opportunities

Food First seeks volunteers to assist with research, education, and outreach at their Oakland, California, office. A minimum commitment of 10 hours per week for 3 months is required.

Contact Information

398 60th Street
Oakland, CA 94618
(510) 654-4400
www.foodfirst.org
foodfirst@foodfirst.org

National Coalition for the Homeless (NCH)

NCH is a national advocacy network for homeless persons, activists, service providers, and others committed to ending homelessness. They sponsor a variety of projects around the issues of housing, economic justice, voting rights, and access to health care, including Kids' Day on Capitol Hill, the Street Newspaper Project, the "You Don't Need a Home to Vote" voting rights campaign, and the Temporary/Day Labor Project. Established in 1984.

Volunteer Opportunities

NCH encourages interested people to seek volunteer opportunities at shelters and direct service agencies in their communities. A partial listing of service providers can be found on the NCH website's directory of local homeless services (www.nationalhomeless.org/local/local.html).

Contact Information

Headquarters:
1012 14th Street NW, Suite 600
Washington, DC 20005-3471
(202) 737-6444
www.nationalhomeless.org
info@nationalhomeless.org

National Mental Health Association (NMHA)

NMHA works to improve the care and health of the 54 million Americans with mental disorders, through advocacy, research, education, and local programs at more than 300 community mental health centers nationwide. Established in 1909.

Volunteer Opportunities

Volunteers are needed to assist callers at the NMHA information center in Virginia. NMHA also utilizes professional and other volunteers to help on mental-health screening days. Additionally, NMHA has volunteer opportunities at 340 local centers nationwide.

Contact Information

Headquarters:
1021 Prince Street
Alexandria, VA 22314-2971
(800) 969-6642
www.nmha.org
infoctr@nmha.org

Planned Parenthood Federation of America, Inc. (PPFA)

PPFA is the world's largest and oldest voluntary family planning organization, dedicated to the principles that "every individual has a fundamental right to decide when or whether to have a child, and that every child should be wanted and loved." Based on these beliefs, Planned Parenthood seeks to provide comprehensive reproductive and complementary health-care services to any person who requests them. Established in 1916.

Volunteer Opportunities

Volunteers at Planned Parenthood may work in a clinic; participate in advocacy, organizing, or outreach; or support the organization in an administrative capacity. Interested individuals should contact their local affiliates for specific opportunities.

Contact Information

Headquarters:
333 Broadway, Third floor
San Francisco, CA 94133
(415) 956-8856
www.plannedparenthood.org

HUMAN RIGHTS

Amnesty International (AI)

Amnesty International is a Nobel Prize–winning worldwide activist organization with more than one million members. AI works to free prisoners of conscience, gain fair trials for political prisoners, abolish the death penalty, and end torture, political killings, and "disappearances" throughout the world. Established in 1961.

Volunteer Opportunities

AI volunteers work in hundreds of community groups across the country and the world. Activities will vary, but may include letter-writing campaigns, demonstrations, and other direct actions. AI also encourages at-home activism through their Freedom Writers Network and Urgent Action Network, for which members make phone calls and send letters, faxes, telegrams, and emails.

Contact Information

Headquarters:
322 Eighth Avenue
New York, NY 10001
(212) 807-8400
www.aiusa.org or www.amnesty.org

Center for Victims of Torture (CVT)

CVT is the first organization of its kind in the United States—a private, nonprofit organization that provides care and rehabilitative services to survivors of politically motivated torture and their families. CVT has pioneered a care program for torture victims and in recent years has expanded its work in research, training, and public policy initiatives advocating for torture survivors worldwide. Established in 1985.

Volunteer Opportunities

CVT welcomes volunteers in the Minneapolis and St. Paul area. Volunteers work directly with clients as ESL tutors, drivers, and community guides. They also need volunteer assistance in the areas of communication, media, development, computer technology, public speaking, writing, and special events. CVT makes an effort to match opportunities with the specific skills and interests of volunteers.

Contact Information

717 East River Road
Minneapolis, MN 55455
(612) 626-1400
www.cvt.org
bwickum@cvt.org

Global Exchange

Global Exchange is a human rights organization dedicated to promoting environmental, political, and social justice around the world. Global Exchange is working on many fronts, including campaigns for political, civil, social, and economic rights, a fair trade program, a California human rights program, a public education program, and Reality Tours (intensive travel seminars which encourage socially responsible travel through education and awareness). Established in 1988.

Volunteer Opportunities

Volunteers are welcome at the San Francisco office to work in a variety of capacities. Long-term, project-based opportunities are available in many programs, including Cuba, Mexico, Palestine, corporate accountability, fair trade, the California human rights program, Democracy Now, Reality Tours, economic rights, or in the development or public education departments.

Contact Information

2017 Mission Street, Suite 303
San Francisco, CA 94110
(415) 255-7296
www.globalexchange.org
info@globalexchange.org

Human Rights Watch (HRW)

HRW attracts media and public attention to human rights abuses world-wide, puts international pressure on abusive governments, and provides up-to-the-minute information about conflicts as they occur. Along with partner organizations, HRW won the 1997 Nobel Peace Prize for their work on the International Campaign to Ban Landmines. Established in 1978.

Volunteer Opportunities

HRW offers volunteer opportunities in their offices in New York, Washington, DC, Los Angeles, San Francisco, London, and Brussels. Volunteers may assist with research, administration, and international communications. Interested individuals should submit a resume and cover letter detailing specific interests to the human resources department at the New York headquarters or a regional office.

Contact Information

Headquarters:
350 Fifth Avenue, 34th floor
New York, NY 10118-3299
(212) 290-4700
www.hrw.org
humanresources@hrw.org

Southern Center for Human Rights (SCHR)

SCHR provides legal representation to people facing the death penalty or confined to prisons in the South. The center also works to protect the civil rights of citizens in confinement, to improve the criminal justice and corrections systems, and to develop innovative and humane solutions to crime. Established in 1976.

Volunteer Opportunities

SCHR primarily utilizes graduate and law student volunteers and other individuals with professional qualifications. Responsibilities may include: locating and interviewing witnesses; locating, obtaining, and organizing documents; gathering statistical data; reading transcripts; organizing files; visiting and interviewing clients; conducting research; responding to requests for information; and attending position hearings. Volunteers are invited to send a resume and cover letter, writing sample, and three references.

Contact Information

83 Poplar Street NW
Atlanta, GA 30303-2122
(404) 688-1202
www.schr.org

> After graduating from Michigan State, I joined VISTA and was placed in program development planning (shirt-and-tie work) in conjunction with a community action agency in Birmingham, Alabama. I worked with little kids in Head Start, taught poetry and history to teens in Upward Bound, helped a nutrition group start a sweet-potato-pie co-op, and worked with a food conspiracy serving a poor neighborhood to get them a grocery store.
>
> It was a valuable learning experience. I was changed in that I went in thinking that, like my dad and uncles, I would be a lawyer, except that I would work as an advocate for the disadvantaged. I left feeling that I should do work with my hands as well as my mind, and that I could help best if I did good work and looked out for the disadvantaged one at a time. I'm thankful for the chance to serve my country this way.
>
> —Jeffrey Weinstein

PEOPLE WITH DISABILITIES

The Arc of the United States

The Arc is an advocacy organization dedicated to improving the lives of people with mental retardation. Established in 1950.

Volunteer Opportunities

Volunteering is organized through more than 1,000 chapters nationwide. Volunteers work directly with clients and assist in special programs, fundraising, and administrative responsibilities.

Contact Information

Headquarters:
1010 Wayne Avenue, Suite 650
Silver Spring, MD 20910
(301) 565-3842
www.thearc.org
info@thearc.org

Best Buddies

Best Buddies provides opportunities for one-on-one friendships and supported employment to people with mental retardation. Established in 1989.

Volunteer Opportunities

Best Buddies offers programs for students and citizens that create one-to-one friendships between people with mental retardation and others in the community. Volunteers commit to contact their buddies on a weekly basis, have at least two one-on-one outings per month, and attend chapter meetings and group outings. Volunteers can also be e-Buddies, e-mailing weekly messages for at least one year.

Contact Information

Headquarters:
100 Southeast Second Street, Suite 1990
Miami, FL 33131
(305) 374-2233
www.bestbuddies.org

Bread & Roses

Bread & Roses provides more than 500 live entertainment shows a year to people living in Bay Area institutions. Established in 1974.

Volunteer Opportunities

Bread & Roses welcomes volunteers who would like to perform for people living in Bay Area institutions. They also seek volunteers to host events and help in their office.

Contact Information

233 Tamalpais Drive, Suite 100
Corte Madera, CA 94925-1415
(415) 945-7120
www.breadandroses.org
info@breadandroses.org

National Alliance for the Mentally Ill (NAMI)

NAMI provides education and supports research about brain disorders, and advocates for the rights to adequate health care, housing, counseling, and employment for people with severe mental illnesses. Established in 1979.

Volunteer Opportunities

Interested individuals can volunteer through the national office or through state or local affiliates. NAMI utilizes volunteers to provide information, referrals, and support to callers through the NAMI HelpLine. Volunteers also participate in advocacy, community outreach, education programs, and support groups.

Contact information

Headquarters:
Colonial Place Three
2107 Wilson Boulevard, Suite 300
Arlington, VA 22201-3042
(800) 950-NAMI or (703) 516-7227 (TTY)
www.nami.org

Rose Resnick Lighthouse for the Blind

Rose Resnick Lighthouse for the Blind promotes the independence and empowerment of blind and visually impaired people through a wide range of resources and programs including braille transcription, computer training, employment services, mobility services, and social, educational, and recreational programs. Established in 1902.

Volunteer Opportunities

Many volunteer opportunities are available at this San Francisco–based organization: Personal Service Volunteers provide companionship and assistance to visually impaired people (a minimum commitment of 2 to 3 hours a week for 6 months); volunteers can read the news over the radio as part of Broadcast Services for the Blind; they can work as counselors at the Enchanted Hills Camp in Northern California (summer sessions range from 4 to 12 days each); and they can record themselves reading books, magazines, newsletters, and manuals at home (a commitment of two recording projects per 6-month period is required). There are similar Lighthouses in many U.S. cities; however, these are not directly affiliated with the Rose Resnick Lighthouse, which only serves communities in Northern California.

Contact Information

214 Van Ness Avenue
San Francisco, CA 94102
(415) 431-1481 ext. 271 or (415) 431-4572 (TTY)
www.lighthouse-sf.org

Special Olympics

Special Olympics offers year-round sports training and competition to more than one million people with mental and physical handicaps, worldwide. Established in 1963.

Volunteer Opportunities

Special Olympics relies heavily on volunteers. Volunteers can assist with training (coaching, assisting, working at sports camps), competition and event organizing, school outreach, fund-raising, public relations, and serving on local boards, among other opportunities.

Contact Information

Headquarters:
1325 G Street NW, Suite 500
Washington, DC 20005
(202) 628-3630
www.specialolympics.org
info@specialolympics.org

During my year of community service, I worked as a volunteer coordinator for the Cal Reads program at Malcolm X Elementary School. In addition, I participated in educational workshops that improved my leadership skills. I worked on service projects that included cleaning up an Oakland homeless shelter, weeding and seeding plants in a community garden, restoring computers for youth, and participating in the upkeep of an alternative high school. The end of the year brought me to a juvenile correction facility where my partner and I helped start a library and led book talks encouraging children to read.

This year was more than a list of activities, workshops, and service projects. I gained leadership experience and skills that are not taught in school. I was able to meet people, and ultimately friends, from all walks of life, all united in our strong ethic of service. In addition, I received an educational stipend that helped pay off some of my school loans. Most importantly, behind each of the service projects were people's lives that we touched along the way. In the grand scheme of things we may have made only a small difference, but when people are out there volunteering, a foundation of hope and community takes root.

—Sup Thanasombat

SENIORS

Alzheimer's Association

The preeminent private funder of Alzheimer's studies in the United States, the Alzheimer's Association is a coalition of more than 200 local chapters dedicated to the elimination of Alzheimer's disease through research, and to improved care for people living with the disease. Established in 1980.

Volunteer Opportunities

Alzheimer's Association encourages volunteers to contribute through local chapters.

Contact Information

Headquarters:
919 North Michigan Avenue, Suite 1000
Chicago, IL 60611
(800) 272-3900 or (312) 335-8700
www.alz.org
info@alz.org

Experience Corps

Experience Corps creates opportunities for older adults to provide emotional and academic support to at-risk young people in their communities. Established in 1995.

Volunteer Opportunities

Volunteers can tutor and/or mentor children in need in schools and at community organizations. A minimum commitment of 15 hours a week for one school year is required. Experience Corps is operating in 15 cities across the United States.

Contact Information

Civic Ventures
425 Second Street, Suite 601
San Francisco, CA 94107
(415) 430-0141
www.experiencecorps.org
info@civicventures.org

Little Brothers—Friends of the Elderly

A national organization designed to offer one-on-one companionship for
elderly people. Established in 1946.

Volunteer Opportunities

Volunteers can be matched with a senior for a one-on-one friendship (a
one-year commitment is required). Volunteers are also welcome to assist
at parties, act as drivers, visit seniors during the holidays, help in the
offices, or perform at program-sponsored parties. Interested individuals
should contact one of the offices in Boston, Chicago, Cincinnati,
Houghton (Michigan), Miami, Minneapolis, Omaha, Philadelphia, or San
Francisco.

Contact Information

Headquarters:
954 West Washington Boulevard, Fifth floor
Chicago, IL 60607
(312) 829-3055
www.littlebrothers.org
national@littlebrothers.org

Meals on Wheels Association of America (MOWAA)

Meals on Wheels is a national umbrella organization representing a wide
range of community-based home-delivery and congregate food-service
organizations. Established in 1954.

Volunteer Opportunities

MOWAA encourages interested individuals to volunteer at food delivery
programs in their community.

Contact Information

Headquarters:
1414 Prince Street, Suite 302
Alexandria, VA 22314
(703) 548-5558
www.projectmeal.org

From the fall of 1995 to the summer of 1996, I participated in the AmeriCorps National Civilian Community Corps in Charleston, South Carolina, a residential program that brought together people from all faiths, ethnicities, and backgrounds to do community service. I worked with an ethnically and geographically diverse team of fifteen who became some of the closest friends I have ever had. During my tenure, we helped build trails for the National Historic Trust in Charleston, calculated taxes for the economically disadvantaged in New Orleans, refurbished a public housing development in Washington, DC, and built a boardwalk on the Cumberland Island National Seashore off the coast of Georgia, among many other projects.

The program allowed me to help others, but it also gave me a taste of many cultures, experiences, and professions that I probably wouldn't have been exposed to otherwise. I gained the belief that every person has the right to be respected and should have the chance to give back to his or her community; the experience of bringing about change through service is empowering. I now work with Oxfam America, helping supervise a program for college students working on global issues such as the global AIDS crisis and world hunger. I am very lucky to be able to take the seed and the lesson which was nurtured in me through my AmeriCorps experience and pass it on to others. It is not a responsibility I take lightly.

—Xavier Benavides

National Gray Panthers

Gray Panthers is an intergenerational advocacy group joining people to work on serious social issues such as peace, health care, employment, and housing. Established in 1970.

Volunteer Opportunities

Gray Panthers welcomes volunteers to work on their ongoing campaigns. Volunteers are organized through local affiliates.

Contact Information

Headquarters:
733 15th Street NW, Suite 437
Washington, DC 20005
(800) 280-5362 or (202) 737-6637
www.graypanthers.org
info@graypanthers.org

SOCIAL WELFARE AND EMERGENCY RELIEF

American Red Cross

The American Red Cross provides relief and other services to victims of natural and man-made disasters, as well as to the U.S. armed forces. It has been a pioneer in the areas of nursing, public health, and first aid and safety training. The American Red Cross collects and distributes half of the nation's blood supply. Established in 1881.

Volunteer Opportunities

American Red Cross volunteers are involved in organizing blood drives, teaching first aid and CPR courses, conducting programs for the elderly and youth, delivering emergency messages to members of the military, and working in communities during emergency situations. Volunteer opportunities are arranged by local affiliates.

Contact Information

Headquarters:
431 18th Street NW
Washington, DC 20006
(800) 797-8022
www.redcross.org
info@usa.redcross.org

Catholic Charities USA

Catholic Charities USA is a nationwide social service organization dedicated to helping all people become, and remain, self-sufficient. Services offered include: adoption, child care, counseling, disaster relief, emergency financial assistance, housing assistance, job training, soup kitchens, drug treatment, and youth and elderly services, among others. Established in 1910.

Volunteer Opportunities

Catholic Charities USA supports local chapters working on a wide range of programs and services across the country.

Contact Information

Headquarters:
1731 King Street, #200
Alexandria, VA 22314
(703) 549-1390
www.catholiccharitiesusa.org
info@catholiccharitiesusa.org

Salvation Army

The Salvation Army is a Christian organization dedicated to caring for the poor and others in need. Established in 1878.

Volunteer Opportunities

Volunteers are organized locally to support the Salvation Army in almost all of its activities, including as members of auxiliary groups and advisory organizations, bell-ringers, kitchen and clerical workers, and in special functions during emergency situations.

Contact Information

Volunteer Services Director
1424 Northeast Expressway
Atlanta, GA 30329
(404) 728-1300
www.salvationarmy.org

YMCA (Young Men's Christian Association) of the USA

YMCA is a Chicago-based organization with more than 2,400 local affiliates across the country. The mission of the YMCA is to create a healthy and safe environment for children, as well as to provide services and activities for families and communities. Established in 1851.

Volunteer Opportunities

All local YMCAs are founded and led by volunteers. Opportunities in the following areas may be available (needs vary from one local YMCA to the next): Programming, which includes coaching, babysitting, lifeguarding, and tutoring; Managerial/Consulting, which invites professionals to use their career skills in areas such as architecture, law, medicine, photography, and writing; Support Volunteers, who help keep the YMCA offices operational through bookkeeping, construction, bus driving, secretarial work, answering telephones, and cooking; and Fund-raising, in which volunteers assist with financial campaigns through research, soliciting donations, or working at campaign events.

Contact Information

Headquarters:
101 North Wacker Drive
Chicago, IL 60606
(800) 872-9622 or (888) 333-9622
www.ymca.net

YWCA (Young Women's Christian Association) of the USA

Operating more than 300 facilities across the country, the YWCA is the largest provider of shelter services for women and their families in the country. The YWCA provides child care, shelter, health, fitness, and social justice programs in its effort to empower girls and women and to eliminate racism. Established in 1859.

Volunteer Opportunities

Volunteers work through 324 YWCA facilities across the country. Opportunities include mentoring, fund-raising, program assistance, and membership on boards and committees.

Contact Information

Headquarters:
Empire State Building
350 Fifth Avenue, Suite 301
New York, NY 10118
(212) 273-7800
www.ywca.org

VIOLENCE PREVENTION
AND PEACE

American Friends Service Committee (AFSC)

Founded during World War I to provide service opportunities for conscientious objectors, AFSC is a faith-inclusive Quaker organization committed to social justice and humanitarian service. Today, AFSC focuses on peace and demilitarization, economic and social justice, and youth issues in the United States, Africa, Asia, Latin America, the Caribbean, and the Middle East. Established in 1917.

Volunteer Opportunities

AFSC offers limited volunteer opportunities in international communities. Responsibilities and length of stay will vary according to specific needs. The Quaker Information Center acts as a general resource center for Quaker and non-Quaker volunteer and service opportunities. Visit their website at www.afsc.org/qic.htm or call (215) 241-7024 for detailed information, local contacts, and listings of timely projects.

Contact Information

1501 Cherry Street
Philadelphia, PA 19102
(215) 241-7000
www.afsc.org

Brady Campaign

The Brady Campaign is dedicated to reducing gun violence in America without a complete ban on gun ownership. The campaign works to enact and enforce responsible gun laws and to encourage regulations governing the firearm industry. Established in 1974.

Volunteer Opportunities

Volunteers are used periodically for phone banking, getting out the vote, and performing administrative tasks, depending on need.

Contact Information

Headquarters:
1225 Eye Street NW, Suite 1100
Washington, DC 20005
(202) 898-0792
www.bradycampaign.org

Center for Global Education (CGE)

CGE offers short- and long-term cross-cultural travel opportunities for students and adults. Established in 1982.

Volunteer Opportunities

CGE provides long-term volunteer opportunities to assist with program development and maintenance in Africa and Central and South America.

Contact Information

2211 Riverside Avenue
Minneapolis, MN 55454
(800) 299-8889 or (612) 330-1159
www.augsburg.edu/global/

Council for a Livable World (CLW)

CLW works for a peaceful earth by fighting against weapons proliferation, opposing a national missile defense system, advocating for cuts in military spending and arms exports, and supporting international peacekeeping efforts. Established in 1962.

Volunteer Opportunities

CLW welcomes interns and volunteers in their Washington, DC offices.

While attending high school in Newport Beach, California, I realized early on that public service was beneficial for two reasons: I could satisfy my growing desire to help others and I could score some points with the folks at college admissions. Like many of my classmates, I dove head-first into various projects—a local soup kitchen, a retirement home, a multicultural club, and toy and blood drives.

When I joined AmeriCorps in my second year at UC Berkeley and became a tutor, my view of public service changed drastically. For the first time, I felt serious trepidation at the thought of working with children. How was I to build a relationship with a student whose path to third grade had been so different from my own? I was thrust out of my role as a self-absorbed college student and was forced to learn the principles of classroom management, lesson planning, and literacy education in a matter of weeks. I was also forced to deal head-on with issues of racial and economic inequality and the deficiencies of an underfunded public school system. I was definitely forced out of my comfort zone.

Nothing I have ever heard or read accurately depicts what I experienced on Tuesday and Thursday afternoons in conversation with eight-year-old Elijah. As I got to know my new friend, fears gave way to excitement at the sound of his voice as he bounded through the classroom door. Elijah also began to enjoy our time together and often colored pictures for me. More significantly, his reading speed and comprehension improved considerably by the end of our first semester together, and I could tell he was using some of the techniques I had taught him. My biggest thanks came when Elijah took time to tell me all about his school, his teachers, his hobbies, dreams, and worries.

It perplexes me that I could have gained so much from an effort intended to help someone else, but I suppose this is the nature of meaningful service. I am forever thankful and eager to continue my service to others.

—Matthew B. Singer

Contact Information

110 Maryland Avenue NE, Suite 409
Washington, DC 20002
(202) 543-4100
www.clw.org
clw@clw.org

Nuclear Age Peace Foundation (NAPF)

NAPF works to discover "new ways of thinking and actions that increase the possibilities for peace" while ridding the planet of nuclear weapons. The foundation provides research and education and seeks to influence policy on issues of peace and global survival. Established in 1982.

Volunteer Opportunities

NAPF has many short- and long-term project-based volunteer opportunities out of their Santa Barbara office. Activities range from stuffing envelopes and answering phones to assisting in event organization, writing articles for the website, judging the annual poetry and essay contests, helping train youth speakers, and participating in youth outreach.

Contact Information

PMB 121, 1187 Coast Village Road, Suite 1
Santa Barbara, CA 93108-2794
(805) 965-3443
www.wagingpeace.org
wagingpeace@napf.org

Peace Action

Peace Action (formerly SANE/FREEZE) works to influence policy and encourage activism on peace and demilitarization issues, including reducing military spending, ending the international arms trade, and promoting nuclear disarmament. Peace Action produces a quarterly newsletter with Peace Action Education Fund and also publishes an annual voting record for every member of Congress. Established in 1957.

Volunteer Opportunities

Volunteers are organized through local chapters.

Contact Information

Headquarters:
1819 H Street NW, Suite 420
Washington, DC 20006
(202) 862-9740
www.peace-action.org

Perhaps it is ironic that I associate my first volunteer experience with singer Carly Simon's classic tune "You're So Vain." Playing a static-ridden vinyl version of this song was a Friday afternoon ritual in the special education class at my junior high school in Oak Park, Illinois. Rather than enrolling in home economics or woodshop, I had opted to spend one period each day in this class, playing games with the students and helping them with their end-of-the-day chores. At the ripe age of thirteen, I had taken the first step on a path that has led me to many community service experiences: through the doors of various Habitat for Humanity homes under construction; into the pool with Special Olympics athletes and kids from families with limited financial resources; onto the volunteer staff at a handful of organizations that serve homeless and low-income individuals and families.

Community service is so often deemed to be the ultimate display of altruism. My experience has convinced me that it is much more than that; I always find that I take away as much as, if not more than, I give. My faith in humanity is renewed each time I leave the construction site, the pool, the homeless shelter. I deeply appreciate the infectious nature of community service; many times I have been moved to action by my peers, and I hope that I have been able to do the same for others. In particular, I cherish every moment that I can spend with individuals who have special needs. These interactions have enabled me to fully appreciate the power of nonverbal communication—and to discover that beauty, not to mention action, truly does transcend words.

—Erin Kelley

WOMEN'S RIGHTS

Choice USA

Founded by Gloria Steinem, Choice USA utilizes research, education, leadership training, grass-roots organizing, and media advocacy to promote and protect reproductive choice. Established in 1992.

Volunteer Opportunities

Choice USA primarily employs youth volunteers at their Washington, DC office. Interested adults can get involved staffing voter registration and education tables at music festivals and concerts nationwide.

Contact Information

Headquarters:
1010 Wisconsin Avenue NW, Suite 410
Washington, DC 20007
(888) 784-4494 or (202) 965-7700
www.choiceusa.org
info@choiceusa.org

Equality Now

Equality Now promotes and protects the rights of girls and women around the globe. They have taken action against systematic rape and genocide in Bosnia-Herzegovina, promoted reproductive rights in Poland, brought attention to the trafficking of women in Japan, and condemned female genital mutilation in the many countries where it is practiced. Established in 1992.

Volunteer Opportunities

Equality Now welcomes volunteers for administrative and research tasks in their New York City office.

Contact Information

P.O. Box 20646
New York, NY 10023
(212) 586-0906
www.equalitynow.org
info@equalitynow.org

Global Fund for Women (GFW)

GFW supports the rights of women and girls around the world by providing grants to start and strengthen women's rights groups based outside of the United States. Established in 1987.

Volunteer Opportunities

GFW welcomes volunteers for administrative assistance at their San Francisco office. Volunteers should be able to commit at least 5 hours each week, between 9:00 a.m. and 5:00 p.m., Monday through Thursday. Volunteer orientation meetings are held regularly.

Contact Information

1375 Sutter Street, Suite 400
San Francisco, CA 94109
(415) 202-7640
www.globalfundforwomen.org
volunteer@globalfundforwomen.org

National Abortion and Reproductive Rights Action League (NARAL)

NARAL works to ensure that every woman has access to safe and legal abortion, effective contraceptive options, and quality reproductive health care. They also promote policies that will improve women's overall health and make abortion less necessary. Established in 1966.

Volunteer Opportunities

Volunteers staff information tables at local festivals and community events, get out the vote, canvas, work phone banks, stamp envelopes, attend marches, rallies, and lobby days, and work on electoral strategy, volunteer recruitment, public education, and event coordination. NARAL organizes volunteers through local affiliates and through on-line activist networks.

Contact Information

1156 15th Street NW, Suite 700
Washington, DC 20005
(202) 973-3000
www.naral.org

National Network of Abortion Funds (NNAF)

NNAF is a coalition of abortion funds which provide financial aid in the form of loans and/or grants to low-income women and girls seeking abortions. Established in 1993.

Volunteer Opportunities

NNAF encourages interested individuals to volunteer locally with an abortion fund in their community. Local groups need assistance with duties such as intake, fund-raising, transportation, housing, and general support.

Contact Information

Headquarters:
NNAF c/o CLPP
Hampshire College
Amherst, MA 01002-5001
(413) 559-5645
www.nnaf.org
info@nnaf.org

National Organization for Women Foundation (NOW Foundation)

Allied with the National Organization for Women, the NOW Foundation works for the advancement of women's rights through education, litigation, advocacy, networking, conferences, publications, training, and leadership development. Issues of import include: violence against health clinic workers, violence against women, young feminist outreach, lesbian rights, racial and ethnic diversity, domestic violence, the feminization of poverty, and global feminist issues. Established in 1986.

Volunteer Opportunities

NOW volunteers are organized through local chapters. Volunteers serve on committees, assist with administrative duties, networking, education, and advocacy, and participate in local and regional actions. Volunteer opportunities are also available at the Washington, DC Action Center.

Contact Information

Headquarters:
733 15th Street NW, Second floor
Washington, DC 20005
(202) 628-8669 or (202) 331-9002 (TTY)
www.nowfoundation.org or www.now.org
now@now.org

National Women's Political Caucus (NWPC)

NWPC strives to increase the number of pro-choice women in elected and appointed office, regardless of party affiliation, through economic support and campaign training. Established in 1971.

Volunteer Opportunities

Volunteers work in local and statewide caucuses to promote candidates and advocate for relevant issues.

Contact Information

Headquarters:
1630 Connecticut Avenue NW, Suite 201
Washington, DC 20009
(202) 785-1100
www.nwpc.org
info@nwpc.org

Women in Community Service (WICS)

Established by Church Women United, the National Council of Catholic Women, the National Council of Jewish Women, the National Council of Negro Women, and later, the American GI Forum Women, WICS provides mentoring, job training, and other support services to low-income people nationwide. Established in 1964.

Volunteer Opportunities

WICS welcomes volunteers in its local offices for a variety of activities including fund-raising, mentoring, administrative and public relations assistance, resource development, referrals and counseling, workshop facilitating, and volunteer recruiting. Bilingual volunteers are especially encouraged.

Contact Information

Headquarters:
1900 North Beauregard Street, Suite 103
Alexandria, VA 22311
(800) 442-9427
www.wics.org

As I was growing up in Orange County (California), community service was just something you did between attending school, soccer practices, piano lessons, and ballet classes. For me, community service was working on beach clean-ups and serving at soup kitchens over the holidays. Not until I participated in the AmeriCorps program did I get a sense of what community service really is. As an AmeriCorps member I worked with junior high school students who had fallen below in their reading levels. I recruited volunteers from my own peer group to serve as tutors. I worked with teachers to coordinate lesson plans to suit each student who had fallen behind. Each volunteer was partnered with a student and worked diligently on phonics, grammar skills, and reading strategies.

Community service is much like a double-edged sword. It exposes you to great despair, uncertainty, and hardship; but it is through that uncertainty and hardship that you attain the tools for developing your strength and your will, and affirming your desire to help humankind. What I got out of my involvement in AmeriCorps is the knowledge that within each of us is the ability to make a difference.

—Sandra Sitar

GENERAL RESOURCE ORGANIZATIONS

Corporation for National Service (CNS)

CNS is the umbrella organization for the U.S. government–sponsored AmeriCorps, AmeriCorps*VISTA, the Senior Corps, and Learn and Serve America.

Volunteer Opportunities

Visit their website to be connected with a wide range of volunteer organizations in your area.

See also "AmeriCorps" (p. 22) and "Volunteers in Service to America" (p. 29) under **Community Development and Economic Justice**.

Contact Information

1201 New York Avenue NW
Washington, DC 20525
(800) 942-2677
www.cns.gov

Network for Good

A self-described "ePhilanthropy portal," Network for Good was founded by AOL Time Warner Foundation, the Cisco Foundation, and Yahoo! Inc., in partnership with more than 20 nonprofit foundations and associations. Network for Good is an easy way for interested individuals to learn about causes, donate money, speak out on issues, and find the perfect volunteer opportunity. Established in 2001.

Volunteer Opportunities

An extensive online database can help direct your search by area of interest and location.

Contact Information

www.networkforgood.org

Points of Light Foundation

The foundation encourages citizens to become involved in volunteering and community service as a way to create positive change in society and to connect with others. Established in 1990.

Volunteer Opportunities

Points of Light Foundation works with more than 500 volunteer centers across the country, offering every order of volunteer opportunity.

Contact Information

Headquarters:
1400 I Street NW, Suite 800
Washington, DC 20005
(202) 729-8000
www.pointsoflight.org
www.volunteerconnections.org
info@pointsoflight.org

Part 3:
Policy and Issues Analysis

This section lists organizations that do not offer volunteer opportunities but do provide intelligent, up-to-date information on issues and policies that may be of interest to you.

Alliance for Retired Americans

Founded by a coalition of unions and community groups, Alliance for Retired Americans focuses on issues relevant to retired people, including universal health care coverage, protecting Social Security, and gaining a prescription drug benefit for Medicare users. Established in 2001.

Contact Information

888 16th Street NW, Suite 520
Washington, DC 20006
(888) 373-6497
www.retiredamericans.org

American Psychological Association (APA)

With the largest membership of psychologists in the world, APA works to advance the science of psychology as a benefit to human welfare. Established in 1892.

Contact Information

750 First Street NE
Washington, DC 20002-4242
(800) 374-2721
www.apa.org

Campaign for America's Future

Campaign for America's Future seeks to further a progressive agenda that protects the economic and social rights of all citizens in the face of corporate hegemony. Established in 1996.

Contact Information

1025 Connecticut Avenue NW, Suite 205
Washington, DC 20036
(202) 955-5665
www.ourfuture.org/front.asp
info@ourfuture.org

Campus Outreach Opportunity League (COOL)

COOL encourages college students to embrace activism, get involved in their communities, and become a force for social change. Established in 1984.

Contact Information

37 Temple Place, Suite 401
Boston, MA 02111
(617) 695-2665
www.cool2serve.org
ahoy@cool2serve.org

Center for Community Change (CCC)

With a belief that poor people must lead the effort to eliminate poverty, CCC helps local organizations build their capacity to direct the futures of their communities. CCC provides support in developing strong community leadership, providing critical services, building homes, and developing business. In addition to working at a grass-roots level, CCC has been involved in passing national legislation, including the Community Reinvestment Act and the Home Mortgage Disclosure Act, both of which encourage lending in low-income and minority communities. Established in 1967.

Contact Information

1000 Wisconsin Avenue NW
Washington, DC 20007
(202) 342-0567
www.communitychange.org
info@communitychange.org

Center for Democratic Renewal (CDR)

CDR acts as a national hub for information on hate-group activity and violence. An outgrowth of the National Anti-Klan Network, which was the first multiracial group established to expose and counter hate-group activity, CDR provides an analytical perspective on the social, political, and criminal aspects of hate crimes and hate groups. Through research, public education, leadership training, crisis intervention, community organizing, and technical assistance, CDR has worked with hundreds of communities across the United States to help combat racism, anti-Semitism, religious intolerance, and homophobia. In 2000, CDR formed the Southern Coalition Against Racism and Bigotry (SCARAB), a coalition of southern research and advocacy organizations concerned with racism in the South. Established in 1979.

Contact Information

P.O. Box 50469
Atlanta, GA 30302
(404) 221-0025
www.thecdr.org

Center on Budget and Policy Priorities (CBPP)

CBPP is a research and analysis organization working on public policy issues affecting low- and moderate-income populations. CBPP crunches data and produces analyses meant to be accessible and useful to lawmakers, other nonprofits, and the media. Established in 1981.

Contact Information

820 First Street NE, Suite 510
Washington, DC 20002
(202) 408-1080
www.cbpp.org

Citizens for Tax Justice (CTJ)

CTJ advocates for fair tax laws for ordinary citizens. They support the closing of tax loopholes for corporations and the wealthy, reducing the federal debt, and adequately funding important government programs. Established in 1979.

Contact Information

1311 L Street NW
Washington, DC 20005
(202) 626-3780
www.ctj.org

Coalition on Human Needs (CHN)

CHN is an alliance of organizations working together to promote adequate funding of social services and to ensure that the interests of low-income and vulnerable populations are represented in the national policy debate. Established in 1981.

Contact Information

1120 Connecticut Avenue NW, Suite 910
Washington, DC 20036
(202) 223-2532
www.chn.org
chn@chn.org

Corporation for Supportive Housing (CSH)

CSH helps local organizations create supported housing options for people in need and at risk for homelessness, particularly those coping with extreme poverty, mental and/or physical illness, or addiction. Established in 1991.

Contact Information

50 Broadway, Seventeenth floor
New York, NY 10004
(212) 986-2966 ext. 500
www.csh.org
information@csh.org

CorpWatch

Holding corporations accountable, CorpWatch (formerly known as the Transnational Resource and Action Center) works against corporate-led globalization through education and activism. Past efforts have included playing a role in pressuring Nike to improve the conditions in its overseas sweatshops, and co-producing radio broadcasts from the World Trade Organization meeting and protests in Seattle. A current priority is to redefine the global warming issue as a question of human rights and environmental justice. Established in 1997.

Contact Information

P.O. Box 29344
San Francisco, CA 94129
(415) 561-6568
www.corpwatch.org
cwadmin@corpwatch.org

Disability Rights Advocates (DRA)

DRA works to protect the rights of people with disabilities through research, education, and legal advocacy. Established in 1993.

Contact Information

449 15th Street, Suite 303
Oakland, CA 94612-2821
(510) 451-8644
www.dradvocates.org
general@dralegal.org

Do Something

Do Something provides guidance, resources, support, and encouragement to young people working to better their schools, communities, and country. Established in 1993.

Contact Information

423 West 55th Street, Eighth floor
New York, NY 10019
(212) 523-1175
www.dosomething.org or coach.dosomething.org
mail@dosomething.org

Economic Policy Institute (EPI)

EPI works to include the concerns of middle-income workers in the national discussion on economic policy. EPI provides research and analysis on issues such as trends in wages, incomes, and prices; part-time work; welfare reform; labor market problems; the consumer price index; health care; education; Social Security; Medicare; trade and global finance; jobs and the environment; urban sprawl; and the health of the manufacturing sector, among other areas. Established in 1986.

Contact Information

1660 L Street NW, Suite 1200
Washington, DC 20036
(202) 775-8810
www.epinet.org
epi@epinet.org

Families USA

Families USA is a grass-roots organization working at the local, state, and national level to achieve high-quality, affordable health care for all Americans. Issues of concern include Medicaid, Medicare, managed care, children's health, the uninsured, and communities of color. Established in 1982.

Contact Information

1334 G Street NW
Washington, DC 20005
(202) 628-3030
www.familiesusa.org
info@familiesusa.org

Family Violence Prevention Fund (FVPF)

FVPF works to educate legal and health-care professionals, as well as the public, on the prevalence and effects of domestic violence, and to assist those whose lives are affected by abuse. Established in 1980.

Contact Information

383 Rhode Island Street, Suite 304
San Francisco, CA 94103-5133
(415) 252-8900
www.endabuse.org
info@endabuse.org

Food Research and Action Center (FRAC)

FRAC works to reduce hunger in America through research, advocacy, education, and local program support. Established in 1970.

Contact Information

1875 Connecticut Avenue NW, Suite 540
Washington, DC 20009
(202) 986-2200
www.frac.org

Housing Assistance Council (HAC)

HAC helps rural communities build affordable housing through loans, technical assistance, training, and education. Established in 1971.

Contact Information

1025 Vermont Avenue NW, Suite 606
Washington, DC 20005
(202) 842-8600
www.ruralhome.org
hac@ruralhome.org

Institute on Race and Poverty (IRP)

IRP works to increase dialogue and find solutions for communities constrained by the dual barriers of race and poverty. To that end, the institute seeks to understand race-related poverty and to improve conditions for low-income communities of color through research, advocacy, litigation, and media attention. Established in 1993.

Contact Information

University of Minnesota Law School, 415 Law Center
229 19th Avenue South
Minneapolis, MN 55455
(612) 625-8071
www1.umn.edu/irp

League of Women Voters of America (LWV)

An outgrowth of the suffragist movement, LWV is a nonpartisan grassroots organization that encourages citizens to be involved and informed in the shaping of public policy. Established in 1920.

Contact Information

1730 M Street NW, Suite 1000
Washington, DC 20026-4508
(202) 429-1965
www.lwv.org

NAACP Legal Defense and Educational Fund, Inc. (LDF)

Established by Thurgood Marshall, LDF has been a pioneer in public interest law focusing on education, employment, criminal justice, voting rights, housing, health care, and environmental justice issues as they relate to the African American community. Established in 1940.

Contact Information

Headquarters:
99 Hudson Street
New York, NY 10013
(212) 219-1572
www.naacpldf.org or www.ldfla.org

National Association of Community Health Centers (NACHC)

NACHC provides services and technical assistance to nonprofit community, migrant, homeless, and other health-care centers across the United States. Established in 1970.

Contact Information

1330 New Hampshire Avenue NW, Suite 122
Washington, DC 20036-6300
(202) 659-8008
www.nachc.com

National Center for Bicycling and Walking (NCBW)

NCBW (founded as the Bicycle Federation of America) works to make America a better and safer place to walk and bicycle. NCBW presents informational resources and outlines actions that can be taken to improve the environment for bicycling and walking. They also maintain an Internet Support Center and organize a biennial ProBike/ProWalk Conference. Established in 1977.

Contact Information

1506 21st Street NW, Suite 200
Washington, DC 20036
(202) 463-6622
www.bikewalk.org
info@bikewalk.org

National Congress for Community Economic Development (NCCED)

NCCED is the trade association and advocate for the more than 3,600 community development corporations (CDCs) across the country. CDCs produce affordable housing and create jobs through business and commercial development activities and job training. They also support the growth of light industry and small business, and they encourage affordable housing through new construction and rehabilitation projects. CDCs are owned and controlled by the residents affected by their programs. NCCED serves the industry through public policy research and education, newsletters, other publications, training, conferences, specialized technical assistance, and fund-raising. Established in 1970.

Contact Information

1030 15th Street NW, Suite 325
Washington, DC 20005
(202) 289-9020
www.ncced.org
ncced@ncced.org

National Council of Churches (NCC)

NCC represents 140,000 Protestant, Anglican, and Orthodox congregations across the United States working together to address issues ranging from peace and justice to poverty, racism, the environment, family, and education. Established in 1950.

Contact Information

475 Riverside Drive, Suite 880
New York, NY 10115
(212) 870-2025
www.ncccusa.org
news@ncccusa.org

National Economic Development and Law Center (NEDLC)

NEDLC is a legal and planning resource center fostering economic expansion and social empowerment in low-income communities. NEDLC provides technical assistance, training, research, advocacy, policy formulation, model project development, publishing, and legal services to community groups. Established in 1969.

Contact Information

2201 Broadway, Suite 815
Oakland, CA 94612
(510) 251-2600
www.nedlc.org

National Education Association (NEA)

NEA works at the local, state, and national levels to improve the quality of teaching and learning in America's public schools. Established in 1857.

Contact Information

1201 16th Street NW
Washington, DC 20036
(202) 833-4000
www.nea.org

National Energy Assistance Directors' Association (NEADA)

NEADA represents the state and tribal directors of the Low-Income Home Energy Assistance Program (LIHEAP), which helps almost five million low-income households across the country manage their heating and cooling needs. Established in 1990.

Contact Information

1615 M Street NW, Suite 800
Washington, DC 20006
www.neada.org

National Head Start Association (NHSA)

NHSA is a membership organization supporting 2,400 local Head Start programs across the country (which serve almost one million children nationwide). Head Start is a comprehensive child development program serving low-income children from birth to age 5. Established in 1965.

Contact Information

1651 Prince Street
Alexandria, VA 22314
(703) 739-0875
www.nhsa.org

National Neighborhood Coalition (NNC)

NNC serves as an information center, networking resource, and advocate in Washington, DC for neighborhoods and community-based organizations across the country. Established in 1979.

Contact Information

1030 15th Street NW, Suite 325
Washington, DC 20005
nncnnc@erols.com
(202) 408-8553
www.neighborhoodcoalition.org

Natural Resources Defense Council (NRDC)

NRDC won the passage of the Clean Water Act in 1971 and has been working to ensure a clean and safe environment ever since. With the support of more than half a million members, NRDC works on a wide range of green issues, including the protection of our air, water, wetlands, green spaces, and natural resources; investment in alternative energy sources; and research into environmental health threats. Established in 1970.

Contact Information

40 West 20th Street, Eleventh floor
New York, NY 10011
(212) 727-2700
www.nrdc.org

Ploughshares Fund

Ploughshares Fund contributes money to a wide range of innovative programs—scientific research to media advocacy, lobbying, grass-roots organizing, and education—working toward goals of peace, demilitarization, and nuclear disarmament. Established in 1981.

Contact Information

Fort Mason Center, Building B, Suite 330
San Francisco, CA 94123
(415) 775-2244
www.ploughshares.org

PolicyLink

PolicyLink is a national nonprofit research, communications, capacity-building, and advocacy organization that seeks to enlarge the sphere of influence that affects policy so that community-based organizations are central to the search for solutions. PolicyLink's work is rooted in partnerships with community-building practitioners, national organizations, and others committed to advancing economic and social equity. Established in 1999.

Contact Information

101 Broadway
Oakland, CA 94607
(510) 663-2333
www.policylink.org
info@policylink.org

Population Action International (PAI)

PAI works to provide girls and women around the world with access to family planning and related health services. PAI seeks to influence U.S. and international policy on population issues and to establish connections between reproductive health, population growth, development, and the environment. Established in 1965.

Contact Information

1300 19th Street NW, Second floor
Washington, DC 20036
(202) 557-3400
www.populationaction.org
pai@popact.org

Public Education Network (PEN)

PEN is an association of local education funds working toward public school reform in low-income communities across the country. PEN's goal is to ensure that every child has access to high-quality public education. To that end, the network advocates for a number of issues, including changes in school funding, reevaluation of curriculum and assessment practices, ensuring authority at the school level, ensuring teacher quality at every school, and engaging communities with their local schools. Established in 1983.

Contact Information

601 Thirteenth Street NW, Suite 900 North
Washington, DC 20005
(202) 628-7460
www.publiceducation.org
pen@publiceducation.org

U.S. Action

A national alliance of progressive and grass-roots organizations, U.S. Action seeks to build political muscle behind progressive values and issues. Established in 1999.

Contact Information

1341 G Street NW, Tenth floor
Washington, DC 20005
(202) 661-0216
www.usaction.org
usaction@usaction.org

World Wildlife Fund (WWF)

WWF works to protect endangered species and endangered spaces through a wide range of methods, from strengthening local parks to influencing global environmental policies. Established in 1961.

Contact Information

1250 24th Street NW
P.O. Box 97180
Washington, DC 20090-7180
(202) 293-4800
www.worldwildlife.org

Part 4:
Recommended Readings:
A Novel Approach

The instruction we find in books is like fire. We fetch it from our neighbors, kindle it at home, communicate it to others, and it becomes the property of all.—Voltaire

More often than not, volunteers are placed in communities or neighborhoods that are quite different from their own; asked to work with ethnic, racial, or cultural groups with whom they are unfamiliar; and confronted with problems, issues, and conflicts with which they have little experience. This section is designed to help you to be better volunteers by giving meaning to the old adage "To be forewarned is to be forearmed."

Though classroom learning and the reading of nonfiction can be helpful, they usually tend to be too academic, abstract, and theoretical. They tell you the facts but don't give you psychological, emotional, and moral insight into the complexity and ambiguity of real-life circumstances. Only fiction can give you a sufficient context for understanding these crucial aspects of the human condition. Novels can do wonders for your social vision and moral sensibility—before, during, and after your volunteer experience.

Robert Penn Warren, our first poet laureate, warned us, "History is dying....If this country loses its sense of history, it has lost its sense to complicate men's feelings and emotions. If I could, I would reevaluate the education system in this country, to emphasize history and literature." Warren gets to the heart of the issue: the identity of a society—or a community—is determined by its connection to history and the moral values passed on through its literature. The valuing process is the lifeblood of civilized and human society, necessary for a shared sense of national purpose.

The novelist John Gardner dealt with the same issues in the collection of essays *On Moral Fiction:*

> In a democratic society, where every individual opinion counts, [literature's] incomparable ability to instruct, to make alternatives intellectually and emotionally clear, to spotlight falsehood, insincerity, and foolishness—[literature's] incomparable

ability, that is, to make us understand—ought to be a force
bringing people together, breaking down the barriers of prejudice and ignorance, and holding up ideals worth pursuing.
Literature in America does fulfill these obligations.

Warren and Gardner are absolutely correct. Novels offer genuine
hope for learning how to handle our daily personal problems—and those
of our communities—in a moral and human way. They can help us to
understand the relationship between our inner lives and the outer world
and the balance between thinking, acting, and feeling. They can give us
awareness of place, time, and condition—about ourselves and others. As
our great Nobel Prize winner William Faulkner said, the best literature is
far more true than any journalism.

Throughout history, the imaginations of young people have been
fired by characters who function as role models. Yet when we look
around us today, I'd argue that we find role models who are less than
healthy and truths that are far from self-evident. We find troubling symbols of success, fantasy, or celebrity as, all the while, we are surrounded
by a technology of speed and efficiency that neither questions its means
nor knows its ends. In the past thirty years, mass-marketing and advertising techniques have created an entirely new moral climate in America.
The superficiality, the alienation, the escapism, and the hollowness are a
result of a steady bombardment of confusing and deadening messages
designed to reduce us to passive consumers. And we have paid a heavy
price: a sharp decline in both civic participation and meaningful public
discourse. We have become serious about frivolous issues and frivolous
about serious ones.

How curious: while people around the world are risking their lives
for American democratic ideals, we're voting in underwhelming numbers
and telling pollsters that we're alienated from our political system. Prior
to 9/11, the acquisition of more and more material goods had become
our highest form of endeavor; terminal consumerism had become a way
of life. However, as novelist John Nichols put it, "Thirty-six flavors doth
not a democracy make." How has it come to pass that our founding
fathers gave us a land of political and economic opportunity, and we
have become a nation of political and economic opportunists? As we
have come to worship the idols of power, money, and success, we have
neglected the principles of justice, equality, and community.

Socially conscious novels force us to confront our society's inability
to distinguish between authentic moral behavior and abstract moralizing.
The former is a sensibility, a moral conviction informed by reflection; the
latter is used to manipulate our emotions for self-serving goals. This dis-
tinction is especially critical during a period in which politics has become
entertainment. There is a powerful difference between the glow that illu-
mines and the glare that obscures, between the freedom of imagination
and the slavery of image.

In the face of the awesome power of indiscriminate mass-marketing, American literature has a critical role to play. The job of good literature is to make distinctions, to break the unhealthy grip of phony myths and false symbols, to remind us of human values, to help us feel alive.

We depend on our fiction for metaphoric news of who we are, or who we think we ought to be. The writers of today's social realism are doing no less than reminding us of our true, traditional American values—the hopes, the promises, and the dreams. They know that to point their fingers at the pain of poverty or the hypocrisy of injustice, and to expose false myths and symbols, is an act of allegiance to our nation and to our people.

When we read these novels, we learn about who we are as individuals and as a nation. They inform us, as no other medium does, about the state of our national soul and character—of the difference between what we say we are and how we actually behave. They offer us crucial insights into the moral, social, psychological, and emotional conflicts that are taking place in communities across America. We need such exploration today more than ever.

Dorothy Allison, *Bastard Out of Carolina* (Dutton). An unsparing, passionate, and gritty work about a young girl growing up in poverty. It resonates with integrity, empathy, and realism.

Lisa Alther, *Original Sins* (Knopf). Set in the sixties South, this intelligent and absorbing story details the challenges, dreams, and follies of the era. The novel transcends the differences between races in an insightful and generous manner.

Harriet Arnow, *The Dollmaker* (Avon). A family moves from the hills of Kentucky to industrial Detroit. This epic novel tests the strength of the human heart against the bitterest odds.

James Baldwin, *Another Country* (Dell). A magnificent, tumultuous, and disturbing work about racism that rings with authenticity.

Russell Banks, *Continental Drift* (Ballantine). An absorbing story about a frost-belt family that moves to Florida to find the good life. Instead they find a nightmare.

Charles Baxter, *Shadow Play* (Norton). The assistant city manager of a small, depressed town in Michigan see his life fall apart when the chemical plant he lured to town turns out to be an environmental disaster.

Wendell Berry, *The Memory of Old Jack* (Harvest). Remarkable and graceful, set in Appalachia, offering keen insights into the life of an aging farmer and America's changing values.

Dorothy Bryant, *Confessions of Madame Psyche* (Ata). The twentieth century as experienced by a Chinese American woman. This moving account of Mei-li Murrow's saga is a metaphor for California's and our nation's multicultural experience.

Sandra Cisneros, *The House on Mango Street* (Knopf). A poignant coming-of-age novel set in the Latino section of Chicago with unforgettable characters.

E.L. Doctorow, *Ragtime* (Penguin). A rich and lyrical account of America's social history in the early twentieth century. It dramatically captures the spirit of the country.

Michael Dorris, *A Yellow Raft in Blue Water* (Warner). Compassionate and psychologically complex, this novel spans three generations of Native American women in the Pacific Northwest—on and off the reservation—who share a fierce independence and a love of family.

Ralph Ellison, *The Invisible Man* (Vintage). The powerful classic about race, individuality, and identity. A southern black man moves to New York and learns the many ways whites are unable to see him.

Gretel Ehrlich, *Heart Mountain* (Penguin). Explores the experience of Japanese Americans exiled to a relocation camp in Wyoming and their relationship with local ranchers.

Louise Erdrich, *Love Medicine* (Harper Perennial). Stunning and haunting insight into life for today's Native Americans, on and off the reservation.

Denise Giardina, *The Unquiet Earth* (Ivy). From the devastation of the Depression to the hope of the War on Poverty, this is a moving story of a West Virginia community's struggle for survival.

Kaye Gibbons, *Ellen Foster* (Algonquin). An exhilarating and endearing tale of an eleven-year-old orphan who calls herself "old Ellen," moving from one woebegone situation to another with spirit and determination.

Davis Grubb, *Shadow of My Brother* (Zebra). Perfectly paced, a dramatic tale of a Tennessee town in the 1950s caught in a moral crisis over racial violence.

Ernest Herbert, *The Dogs of March* (New England Press). Brilliant, sensitive, and funny, this novel captures what it is like to be unemployed in the 1980s. Set in New England, it's the American dream gone belly-up.

Linda Hogan, *Mean Spirit* (Ivy). A magical and compelling story about whites robbing the Osage Indian tribe of their oil wealth in Oklahoma.

John Irving, *The Cider House Rules* (Bantam). A fine writer brings his incisive storytelling gifts to fruition with this excellent novel about choice, class, and Yankee common sense.

Arturo Islas, *The Rain God* (Avon). A Southwestern classic set in a fictional small town on the Texas-Mexico border. It examines the spirit of Mexican American life—faith, family, and culture—and how it conflicts with the Anglo drive of "making it."

William Kennedy, *Ironweed* (Penguin). Pulitzer Prize winner's shrewd study of the diceyness of fate. This modern Dante's *Inferno* about life on skid row is especially poignant as homelessness casts a shadow across our land.

Barbara Kingsolver, *Animal Dreams* (Harper Perennial). A wonderful tale of multiculturalism in Arizona, about authenticity, community, integrity, and truth.

Maxine Hong Kingston, *The Woman Warrior: Memories of a Girlhood Among Ghosts* (Vintage). Brilliant and haunting account of the Chinese American experience. Kingston's account of growing up Asian and poor adds a cultural richness to the landscape.

Ella Leffland, *Rumors of Peace* (Harper Perennial). A fierce California girl comes of age during World War II, making her own sense of racism, Nazism, the bombings of Pearl Harbor and Hiroshima, and the coming of peace.

Thomas Mallon, *Henry and Clara* (Ticknor & Fields). Clara and Henry, the young couple in the box with Lincoln when he was shot, are the focus of this riveting account of the political and cultural conflicts of the Civil War era.

Carson McCullers, *The Heart is a Lonely Hunter* (Bantam). This enduring masterpiece, set in small-town Georgia, is a compassionate study of how people confront the problems of poverty, race, class, and gender, and, most important, how they handle the conflicts of the human condition.

Toni Morrison, *Beloved* (Plume). Winner of a Pulitzer Prize, this is a powerful story of the legacy of slavery. The basic theme, that of the relationship between slave and master, examines the tragic complications underlying our historical experience.

Bharati Mukherjee, *The Middleman* (Fawcett). Winner of the National Book Critics Circle Award, this is a profound, intelligent, and often funny book about recent immigrants to America and their struggle to survive.

Faye Ng, *Bone* (Harper Perennial). In a clear and emotionally powerful novel, Ng takes us into the heart and inner secrets of a family in San Francisco's Chinatown.

John Nichols, *The Milagro Beanfield War* (Ballantine). Provides no-nonsense insights into how the economic and political "shell game" is being run on ordinary Americans. Part of the author's New Mexico trilogy, it is a contemporary *Grapes of Wrath*, with Mark Twain's down-home humor.

Joyce Carol Oates, *Them* (Vanguard). A poignant account of the hopes, strategies, and chaos of urban community organizing during the time of the 1960s riots.

Tillie Olsen, *Yonnondio* (Laurel). A remarkable, poetic, and timeless book about a young family's struggle to overcome poverty during the Great Depression.

Ruth L. Ozeki, *My Year of Meats* (Penguin). A feisty Japanese American filmmaker takes on the beef industry, chemical corporations, and commercial advertising in this witty, provocative, muckraking novel.

Jayne Anne Phillips, *Machine Dreams* (Dutton). A chronicle of mid-American family life, from the Depression to Vietnam, about identity, shifting values, and the ironies of a rapidly changing America.

Marge Piercy, *Gone to Soldiers* (Fawcett). A sweeping epic of women's lives during World War II that seamlessly blends political, social, and economic issues on the home front.

Chaim Potok, *Davita's Harp* (Fawcett). A compassionate coming-of-age novel about a young New York girl developing a social, moral, and political consciousness.

E. Annie Proulx, *Postcards* (Collier). Winner of the Pen/Faulkner Award. Proulx has written a remarkable story of the struggle of New England farmers to confront the loss of home and place in economic hard times.

May Sarton, *Kinds of Love* (Norton). This book is about truth, honesty, integrity—all those traditional virtues that have become unfashionable. Three generations celebrate the American bicentennial in a small town in New Hampshire.

Danzy Senna, *Caucasia* (Riverhead). Birdie Lee's black father flees in the seventies, and her white, activist mother is forced to take the girl underground, where Birdie copes with adolescence and the complexities of her racial identity.

Mary Lee Settle, *The Scapegoat* (Ballantine). A stirring account of a historic strike in the coal fields, this novel describes the real-life struggle between immigrants (Italian, Greek, Polish, Slavic, among others) and robber barons. You won't find this in most history texts.

Jane Smiley, *Moo* (Random House). The financial, academic, sexual, and political scandals of a Midwestern university are laid bare in this satire of higher education.

John Steinbeck, *The Grapes of Wrath* (Penguin). This classic novel of farmers forced to move West during the Great Depression electrified the nation and reminded us of our historical commitment to compassion, opportunity, and social justice.

Kurt Vonnegut, *Jailbird* (Dell). An unflinching mix of wit, politics, and class. Vonnegut's hilarious tale about Nixon's social policies of "benign neglect" and the Watergate era should be required reading.

Alice Walker, *Meridian* (Fawcett). A powerful novel about civil rights activism in the South in the sixties. Warm, generous, and complex, Walker's book challenges each of us to examine what it is to become a decent, responsible, and honorable person.

Index of Organizations

About the Author

Arthur I. Blaustein teaches community development, social history, and urban policy at the University of California, Berkeley. His most recent book is *The American Promise—Equal Justice and Opportunity*. He was chair of the President's National Advisory Council on Economic Opportunity under President Jimmy Carter and in 1996 received the John Dewey Award for Distinguished Public Service. Professor Blaustein presently serves on the board of the National Endowment for the Humanities (appointed by President Bill Clinton) and has been the faculty advisor to the AmeriCorps program at UC Berkeley for the past six years.

Other books by Arthur Blaustein:

The American Promise—Equal Justice and Opportunity (editor)
Man Against Poverty: World War III (editor, with Roger Woock)
The Star-Spangled Hustle (with Geoffrey Faux)
The New War on Poverty (editorial advisor)